1 0 S T E P S T O

Successful Teams

■ ■ ■ ■ ■ ■ ■ ■ ■ ■

Renie McClay

ASTD
PRESS

Alexandria, Virginia

ASTD Press is an internationally renowned source of insightful and practical information on workplace learning and performance topics, including training basics, evaluation and return-on-investment, instructional systems development, e-learning, leadership, and career development. Visit us at www.astd.org/ASTDPress.

Ordering information: Books published by ASTD Press can be purchased by visiting our website at store.astd.org or by calling 800.628.2783 or 703.683.8100.

Library of Congress Control Number: 2009920425
ISBN-10: 1-56286-675-3
ISBN-13: 978-1-56286-675-4

ASTD Press Editorial Staff:
Director of Content: Dean Smith
Manager, ASTD Press: Jacqueline Edlund-Braun
Senior Associate Editor: Tora Estep
Senior Associate Editor: Justin Brusino
Copyeditor: Pamela Lankas
Indexer: Mary Kidd
Proofreader: IGS
Interior Design and Production: International Graphic Services
Cover Design: Ana Ilieva Foreman

Printed by Versa Press, Inc. East Peoria, Illinois,
www.versapress.com

1 0 S T E P S T O S U C C E S S

Let's face it, most people spend their days in chaotic, fast-paced, time- and resource-strained organizations. Finding time for just one more project, assignment, or even learning opportunity—no matter how career enhancing or useful—is difficult to imagine. The *10 Steps* series is designed for today's busy professional who needs advice and guidance on a wide array of topics ranging from project management to people management, from business strategy to decision making and time management, from stepping in to deliver a presentation for someone else to researching and creating a compelling presentation as well as effectively delivering the content. Each book in this ASTD series promises to take its readers on a journey to basic understanding, with practical application the ultimate destination. This is truly a just-tell-me-what-to-do-now series. You will find action-driven language teamed with examples, worksheets, case studies, and tools to help you quickly implement the right steps and chart a path to your own success. The *10 Steps* series will appeal to a broad business audience from middle managers to upper-level management. Workplace learning and human resource professionals along with other professionals seeking to improve their value proposition in their organizations will find these books a great resource.

C O N T E N T S

PREFACE

I believe teams can accomplish anything and are vital to the success of organizations. I also think many organizations take teams for granted. They take people who are already busy and overworked and put them on a team to solve a business problem. The team doesn't necessarily get the guidance or resources it needs, and it certainly doesn't get the recognition and reward it deserves. I hope that by reading this book team leaders can pick up some pointers and team members will be inspired to try some new tools to help with the effectiveness and efficiency of their teams.

It seems fitting that this book on teams required a team effort. The book is a result of experience gained working in the corporate world, building client teams, and conducting research, coupled with experiences and contributions of peers and colleagues. Several individuals made significant contributions to this book and I would like to thank them by name: Deborah Taber, whose work with corporate teams and leaders with many organizations filled an important void; Lanie Jordan, whose experience leading teams and constant "what can I do to help" attitude was a large blessing throughout this project; Trish Uhl, whose virtual teaming experience provided a much-needed perspective for the book; Ken Phillips, who is a performance management guru and was kind enough to share his wonderful team assessments; and Louann Swedberg, a great writing resource, who helped to turn individual contributions into a whole product—and was still friendly at the eleventh hour of the deadline!

In addition, I would like to acknowledge the following people who made significant contributions: Jerry Acuff, Sarah Miller Caldecott, Terrence Donahue, Cary Dudczak, Maria Edelson, Gerald Haman, Teresa Hiatt, Catherine Marienau, Fiona Odumosu, Bob Rickert, Leodis Scott, Amy Tupler, and Rick Wills.

We worked virtually and we celebrated virtually with a toast (I'm not talking about wheat toast). Many thanks. These are great peers, friends, and teammates.

INTRODUCTION

Teams, and work groups working together as a team, will continue to be critical to business success. The global nature of business today demands that people work well with others who are often far away and from different cultures. This adds a new dimension for many managers and leaders as well as for many team members.

Teams need to be able to connect with each other quickly as teammates determine what needs to be done, identify obstacles and overcome them, and meet deadlines and goals. Positive collaboration becomes an important part of the team's work.

Coming from a background in sales and having experience with several *Fortune* 500 companies, I have worked on some truly remarkable teams. My favorite were teams in which people became friends and worked through problems. In these environments we helped each other out and were very goal focused. No one harbored hidden agendas, or if someone did, the team called him or her on it.

I have gathered the teachings of seasoned colleagues who have been successful at working in team environments and incorporated them here so that you can benefit from their lessons learned and apply them to your own teams—whether you are leading a team or participating on one.

What You'll Find in This Book

This book was written for both team leaders and team members. Each step has content and specific tips intended for both audiences. This is no accident. Team leaders must lead transparently so the team members know exactly what is happening. But great teams are composed of both effective leaders and effective team members. This book can be used by team members individually or by the entire team as a team-building and developmental tool. There are assessments, tips, and tools included for both audiences.

You will find this book to be a short and sweet resource on the topic of successful teams. It is not an exhaustive study of teams; rather, it is meant to be a quick read with steps that are easily implemented and contain the essential keys to team success. You can read it as 10 steps that build on each other or you can go directly to the step that interests you and solves today's problem.

Here are the 10 steps that I believe are necessary to build successful teams:

Step 1: Identify Team Leaders with Enthusiasm, Energy, and Vision—Creating the team is perhaps the single most important step in the process. If the team doesn't possess the right skills and drive to accomplish the goals, then the work will be painful and often unsuccessful. The right leader can either help or hinder the process.

Step 2: Ensure Roles Are Clarified and Understood—If team member roles are not clear, one of two things will happen. The team will be inefficient because time will be wasted as more than one person does the same thing. Or, the team will be ineffective, because something important won't get done at all. Clarifying who is responsible for what is critical up front.

Step 3: Create an Environment to Encourage Communication—Healthy and effective communication builds trust. Giving positive and constructive feedback helps to keep things on track and eliminate errors. Managing conflict helps a team focus on the goal rather than on interpersonal dynamics that can slow things down and deteriorate the morale of the team.

Step 4: Build Strong and Effective Relationships—Getting to know the other team members is one of the most important parts of building morale on the team. The members are not robots, and they need to get to know each other as human beings. When relationships are strong, relational tension will be weak, and people can focus on the work to be done.

Step 5: Build Processes to Track Progress and Get Things Done—Building processes and tracking progress are necessary for many reasons. This step builds efficiencies that allow a team to replicate its success. It also helps to keep stakeholders informed and team members aware of what is happening now and what needs to happen next.

Step 6: Assess the Team Regularly for Top Performance—Ideally, everyone needs to be aware of his or her strengths and then support fellow team members' development efforts. A leader who knows who needs support is a beautiful thing. No one possesses every skill and all knowledge, so self-awareness is helpful for the team's progress and ultimate growth and success.

Step 7: Tap Into Creative Energy of the Team for Innovative Approaches—A team can continue to do things the way it has always done them, but it can be energizing to develop creative solutions. Creativity and innovation can save time and money. Teams can be innovative about the end product or about how the team operates. A mix of left- and right-brain thinking can also be very powerful in the team environment.

Step 8: Use Virtual Team Techniques Effectively—Working remotely and participating on a team virtually is often challenging. Connecting with people you may never have met can make it harder to build trust and learn to rely on team members. Dependable technology and deliberately cultivating people skills can help to smooth out this step.

Step 9: Deal with Team Problems and Move On—All teams face problems. Perhaps the single most important quality of a team is how it works through problems. This step identifies 10 different problem areas that many teams experience and gives tips on solving them.

Step 10: Reward and Celebrate Success—Many teams do not celebrate victories. Many organizations do not properly reward team successes. There are ways to reward teams that do not cost much and there are even some that cost nothing. If a team is making a significant contribution to the organization, it should get more than an email saying thanks. This step explores ways to recognize the contributions.

This book was written to be a very practical resource. Enjoy it and use it to be a stronger team member and to strengthen your team!

Form the Team— Identify Leaders with Enthusiasm, Energy, and Vision

OVERVIEW

What is a team?

Types of teams

What teams do for the organization

Members of the team

Stages of team development

Keys to success

Teamwork is a journey and not a destination.

—Kimberley Cornwell

Teams have been around since the beginning of recorded history. People have always worked together for a common goal. Take military squadrons, sports teams, orchestras, and bands, for example. The entire foundation of teamwork is based on the belief that the whole is greater than the sum of its parts and that together we can accomplish more than we can by working independently.

In most organizations at work today, just about every group is referred to as a team. All too often, managers want to call their department's employees a "team" as a way to inspire the concept of team building. A word to the wise: Employees are rarely fooled! In truth, not all business issues are best addressed by the formation of a team. So, which situations need teams? What *is* a team? And, how will you, as a manager or leader, know if you have an *effective* team? Let's begin by looking at the definition of team.

What Is a Team?

Webster's Dictionary defines the word "team" as "a group of people associated together to work on or achieve a common goal or purpose." Though this may not always be the case, it is generally understood that teams pull together and that team members support each other and are collectively accountable for the work they produce.

Most teams have two things in common: They have coaches (or leaders) and players (or team members). Coaches, whose job it is to inspire the team, set the ground rules, monitor progress, and get out of the way so the teams can run the play and score the goal. The coaches, simply put, are the team leaders and facilitators. Players consist of the team members who communicate, collaborate, solve problems, and run the various plays to ensure specific tasks get accomplished and a successful outcome is achieved.

Teams share several common characteristics:
- The work and the outcomes are connected in a way that differs from the way that individual contributors operate. Team members are more interconnected and interdependent.
- Team members share accountability for the process and the results.
- There is a sense of shared commitment in the way that members interact and agree to work together to produce their end products.

The question was posed earlier about how you know if you have an *effective* team. So, in addition to the characteristics above, winning teams share these skills and abilities:

- communicate clearly
- are accountable
- are action oriented
- use effective listening
- are goal oriented
- use a participative decision-making style
- employ problem-solving skills and techniques
- are cross-culturally sensitive
- look beyond their own needs
- leverage conflict-management tools
- develop cooperative relationships
- relate well with management
- inspire trust.

Types of Teams

There are many different types of teams in our society today. We will focus our discussion on teams operating in business organizations, such as executive teams, department teams, short-term or ad hoc process-improvement teams, longer-term self-directed teams, and permanent functional teams that span multiple departments. And, in today's work environment, virtual teams operating across time zones and continents are becoming increasingly commonplace. (Much more discussion is given to virtual teams in Step Eight.)

There are two key types of teams in business: independent teams and cross-functional teams. When forming a team, consider the type of team you need to accomplish the desired task.

Independent teams are self-managed. Each person works independently on the same task for the greater good of the team. Think of the "scramble" format used in golf. Each of the players hits a tee shot, and then the best shot hit by one of the group members is selected. The whole team then moves and each member drops his/her ball and plays from that location on the fairway. Players don't keep an individual score, they work for the good of the team.

Cross-functional teams are made up of members who have different expertise who often come from other areas of the business and all work together toward the common goal. Usually each team member performs separate tasks. A good example of this may be seen in a marching band where each member plays a different instrument simultaneously and works toward the common goal through a collaborative effort. In a cross-functional team, various departments often are represented to ensure they achieve an organization's mission.

What Teams Do for the Organization

Organizations that use teams effectively to work through goals or operational challenges accomplish much more than simply solving an internal problem, they create a culture of self-motivated problem-solvers. According to Deborah K. Taber, an organizational development consultant who has been coaching corporate teams for over 20 years, "While teams may not be the solution to every business problem, they can accomplish many significant things." She points out that teams

◆ *Are the Best Organizational Change Agents*—
Organizational change is inevitable. The old adage that people don't mind the change as much as they mind having to be changed reflects the compelling truth that senior executives cannot effectively mandate or implement change. If an organization wants to reduce the amount of resistance to a proposed change, it should entrust several teams of employees to develop recommendations for the change and begin implementing them.

◆ *Form Partnerships to Solve Operational Problems*—
Effectively trained employee teams know what's what. They know what the customer service issues are and how to reduce costs and service errors, they know how to decrease lead times and cycle times on the shop floor, they know how to best manage the work processes, they know

what the problems are with the raw materials and where to find the lost supplies. Over the course of the last two decades we have come to understand that employees, not managers, are often the real experts on what is really happening on the front lines.

◆ **Network to Problem Solve**—Whether a team is formed from within a department or spans multiple departments, teams of employees already know who to talk to in adjoining departments regarding errors or omissions in the work process. Barriers often fall away when employee teams feel empowered to search out the source of their existing work problems.

Members of the Team

Teams are made up of individuals who play different roles. As mentioned, the main distinction in team roles is between the team leader and the team members. Let's look at each role, beginning with the team leader.

Team Leaders maintain a constant balance between keeping the group on task, on the one hand, and allowing the team to make its own decisions on the other. Leaders are charged with keeping the team motivated and moving forward to accomplish its task. The best leader may or may not be a supervisor or manager of the group. Effective leaders never use positions of power to push their agendas. Team leaders communicate team progress with others, act as a coach when rules aren't being adhered to, become a cheerleader to encourage progress, and celebrate personal as well as team accomplishments.

Team Members participate and dedicate themselves to the team mission. Team members must be honest and have the ability to listen to others' perspectives. It is not necessary to be a subject matter expert to be an effective team member. It is crucial that team members place their own agendas by the wayside for the good of the team. Great team members are often successful problem solvers. They often see opportunity where others see issues. Team members are bound together by mission, respect, and the realization that together they can work to achieve the mission.

The leaders who work most effectively, it seems to me, never say "I." And that's not because they have trained themselves not to say "I." They don't think "I." They think "we"; they think "team." They understand their job to be to make the team function. They accept responsibility and don't sidestep it, but "we" gets the credit. This is what creates trust, what enables you to get the task done.

—Peter Drucker

Choosing a Team Leader

Great care should be given to the selection of team leaders. They a crucial role in the success of the team by understanding and continually reinforcing the team's vision. Also, team leaders have myriad team responsibilities—often in addition to their regular job duties. When determining who should fill this role, you will need to select individuals whose regular duties can be reduced or shifted elsewhere for a defined period of time while they are serving as a team leader.

It is important that the team leader directs the initial activities of forming the team, helping members learn new skills, and setting up the team's mission, focus, and process. It is equally important that the team leader allow the team members to share responsibilities for problem solving and accomplishing project tasks. The team leader should never try to maintain complete control over the team throughout the course of the team project.

Team leader responsibilities include

◆ scheduling and facilitating team meetings

◆ coordinating processes for the team

◆ serving as the liaison between the team and the rest of the organization

◆ coaching and moderating team members if and when there are any differences of opinion or personality clashes

◆ communicating effectively at all levels of the organization—in both written and verbal formats

◆ articulating the team's vision continuously and facilitating the vision's translation into action clearly enough for the team to stay motivated and on target

◆ serving as a liaison between the team members and any other team or committee

◆ coaching team members in building or strengthening skills.

The *skills* needed for the team-leader role can vary greatly from team to team and project to project. *Competencies,* however, for team leaders remain relatively the same. See

POINTER

Vision is caught, not taught. People respond to vision.

—*Terrence Donahue*

POINTER

On Team Leaders

Great team leaders are servant leaders. They see and hear between the lines of communications. They are intuitive, proactive, and great problem solvers. They recognize when a team member is struggling with personal issues versus with professional issues and skillfully address the issues with empathy and consideration.

—*Sue Drake*

the pointer for an overview of common competencies required for this role.

Leading Versus Managing

Sometimes there is confusion about the difference between leading a team and managing a group. A quote from a trusted colleague, Donald Sandel, summarizes this difference best (see pointer).

Another way to look at this distinction is shown in Table 1.1.

If you find yourself in a leadership role, use Checklist 1.1 to see if you are doing what it takes to be effective in leading your team. If you answer "no" to any of these questions, you may want to renew your efforts to change the answer to "yes"!

Choosing Team Members

Ideally, the organizational sponsor (if there is one) and the team leader should identify the various departmental areas and skills needed for representation on the team. It is important to have all areas affected by the team's project represented on the team. A

Team Leader Competencies

A team leader values:

◆ collaboration vs. individual contribution
◆ creative problem solving and innovation by supporting and initiating new ideas, methods, and solutions of the team.

A team leader demonstrates:

◆ great team-building skills and sensitivity by getting others to work cooperatively
◆ concern for quality by monitoring quality and accuracy of others' work and by personally maintaining high standards of quality
◆ results orientation by focusing on setting and achieving challenging goals for self and others
◆ interpersonal relationship management and communication skills by sharing ideas, opinions, and feelings with others in a way that builds consensus.

A team leader:

◆ uses analytical thinking to identify root causes to problems; uses a logical, sequential approach to problem solving; and weighs costs and benefits of possible solutions
◆ is skilled at breaking down goals and projects into component tasks, gives instruction effectively, and enlists team and organizational resources to accomplish tasks on time.

TABLE 1.1
Managing versus Leading

Management	Leadership
Focuses on the bottom line: "How can I best accomplish things?	Focuses on the top line: "What do I want to accomplish?"
Does things right	Does the right things
Efficiently climbs the ladder of success	Determines whether the ladder is against the right wall

CHECKLIST 1.1
Qualities of a Team Leader

Check the questions to which you can answer "Yes."

- ❐ Do people find you approachable?
- ❐ Do you make yourself accessible?
- ❐ Do you treat people fairly, equally, and with respect?
- ❐ Do you ask for opinions?
- ❐ Do you connect with team members individually as human beings?
- ❐ Do you build a relationship with each person?
- ❐ Do you know what motivates each individual?
- ❐ Do you help the group to manage and resolve conflict?
- ❐ Do you regularly provide feedback and show appreciation?
- ❐ Do you explain the reasons for your decisions?
- ❐ Do you meet commitments?
- ❐ Do you take a personal interest in the team members?
- ❐ Do you have relationships with others in the organization that will be helpful?
- ❐ Do you give everyone a chance?
- ❐ Do you give feedback without judging the individual?
- ❐ Do you stay open to differences?
- ❐ Do you recognize individual contributions as well as group accomplishments?
- ❐ Do you say "Thank you"?

Boxes without checks are potential areas to improve upon to develop your team leader skills.

manageable team size varies, but typically includes between five and eight members. Criteria for team membership might include these considerations:

> Although it is sometimes hard to do, it is crucial that team members place their personal agendas by the wayside for the greater good of the team.

- ◆ All areas affected by the project or by the various stages of the process being examined must be represented.
- ◆ The various levels of employees or management, professions, technical areas, trades, departments, or work areas should all be well represented.
- ◆ Employees who have expressed concern for this issue need to be included. Often, those employees who are most vocal are the informal leaders who will be instrumental in selling the ultimate solutions to other employees.
- ◆ Employees who have good ideas as well as those employees who like to "get things done" make valuable team members.
- ◆ It is better for the team to have employees with different personality "types." Research has shown that teams composed of various types of individuals take longer to reach consensus but ultimately make better decisions than do teams consisting of similar personality types.
- ◆ Employees who can actively learn from mistakes are an asset.

In some cases it may be difficult to include employees and their managers on the same team. Employees may feel intimidated or stifle their opinions with managers present. Consider inviting managers to a particular meeting and asking them to serve as consultants to the team when specific information or technical expertise is needed. There will be situations, however, when both (manager and employee) are needed for a team to be effective. It's

POINTER

Five Stages of Team Development

1. **Forming**—The group explores relationships with other members and determines what behaviors are acceptable.
2. **Storming**—Members begin to participate and influence the team's decisions.
3. **Norming**—The team identifies acceptable ways to interact with each other as members establish norms of acceptable behavior and operation.
4. **Performing**—Individuals begin to work cohesively within their established team expectations and experience success in achieving the team's goals.
5. **Adjourning**—When the team disbands, members evaluate the team's work, document its process, findings, and outcomes, and celebrate the team's efforts.

good to be sensitive to these kinds of issues and have alternatives in mind.

Stages of Team Development

So far we have examined what makes a team, characteristics of a team, how teams affect organizations, and the key roles on a team. Let's turn our attention to the generally accepted stages that teams go through in the process of completing their mission. According to Scholtes, Joiner, and Streible (2003), who wrote *The Team Handbook,* there are five stages of team growth: forming, storming, norming, performing, and adjourning (see pointer).

Some teams progress rapidly through the first four stages in only a few meetings, whereas others struggle and stall in the storming stage for a long time. Sometimes, a team will experience norming or performing in one meeting and fall back into storming at the next meeting. There is no correct formula for progression through the stages of team development. The key is to recognize and respond appropriately to the stage your team is in at any moment.

Keys to Success

Over the years, I've led and been a member of many teams—some worked well and others didn't. From that experience I have found several key elements that are critical to any team's success: trust, shared vision, clear and comprehensive plan, diverse team members, and sustained momentum.

Trust Is a Must

A lack of trust is perhaps the most pervasive problem facing any team. Invariably, team members come to meetings with personality conflicts, competing departmental agendas, and emotional baggage from old feuds. All of these things contribute to a lack of trust and cohesiveness among team members. Individuals working together must be able to trust one another, and that trust is built one interaction at a time.

Trust is a nebulous concept that exists in our minds and is based on perceptions and interpretations of others' behavior. Unfortunately, there is no magic bullet for creating initial trust or rebuilding it among team members once it has been violated. Trust is built by consistently acting with integrity and by continually doing what you say you will. One or two team-building exercises will not repair one or two month's worth of dysfunctional behavior and hurt feelings.

Shared Vision

The main priority in establishing an effective team is to create a shared vision. The initial vision might have been handed down by a senior management team or it could be the product of a fact-gathering process. However the team's mission is developed, the team effort will only be successful if there is a clear understanding of what the team is going to achieve and the scope of the undertaking is clearly defined. Start with a written statement of what the team is expected to accomplish—with any resources available, deadlines, schedules, or constraints clearly listed. Then, discuss the team's vision and determine if it is truly achievable. Appendix A offers tips and tools to use to set a firm foundation at your kick-off meeting.

The team should develop a list of questions and perceived barriers and decide if the scope is too big or inappropriate for this team to handle. It is important to emphasize that all members are encouraged to ask questions about the vision until they are confident that it can be achieved.

Clear and Comprehensive Plan

Once the team's vision is clearly defined, another key to success is to establish a project plan or team action plan. The team members will find that the process of developing and refining the project plan can be a unifying process as long as all members are equally involved in this process. Sharing ideas during the initial action-planning stage allows for the identification of work steps, milestones, and needed resources.

Diverse Team Members

My experience working with many different types of teams suggests that the best and most creative teams are made up of individuals with diverse technical backgrounds and personalities. Although these kinds of teams take longer to get through the storming stage, they tend to see problems and solutions from very different viewpoints and therefore are better, more creative problem-solvers.

Sustained Momentum

Teams often experience many different feelings and emotions throughout the course of the team's work. The initial stage is often one of high expectations and optimism. However, as team members begin to work through the complexities of problem identification, fact gathering, and problem resolution, they can often become discouraged. The "ups and downs" of teaming are to be expected and should be managed by the team leader with a great deal of coaching and patience. Maintaining the team's enthusiasm in the midst of looming deadlines and mounting work is a critical part of a team's success.

Make It Happen!

An important question to ask is: What does a great team look like? Peter Senge, author of *The Fifth Discipline*, describes it as "alignment—when a group of people function as a whole" (Senge 1990). In this state, he continues,

> when a team becomes more aligned, a commonality of direction emerges and individuals' energies harmonize . . . a resonance or synergy develops, like the coherent light of a laser rather than the incoherent and scattered light of a light bulb. There is commonality of purpose, a shared vision and understanding of how to complement one another's efforts. . . . Team learning is the process of aligning and developing the capacity of a team to create the results its members truly desire. (Senge 1990)

Work with your team to find your own sweet spot or rhythm. Get in "alignment" behind your team mission and take your team to the next level.

NOTES:

_____

_____

_____

_____

_____

_____

_____

_____

_____

_____

_____

_____

_____

_____

_____

_____

_____

_____

_____

_____

_____

_____

_____

Ensure Roles Are Clarified and Understood

OVERVIEW

Define and assign team roles

Enhance members' skills and use talents

Focus on the team's strengths

Determine if the team is working

Strike a delicate balance in leadership

Talent wins games, but teamwork wins championships.

—Michael Jordan

Imagine a basketball team in which all the players are great shooters but no one can dribble. You have all this amazing talent and capacity to score, however, you lack the ability to get into position to make the shot and score a goal. How would that team perform? The word "chaos" comes to mind. The same, unfortunately, can hold true for your team unless you pick the right team members with the right strengths. The answer to forming an effective team lies in determining the diverse competencies within each player and putting each in the correct position.

Define and Assign Team Roles

In the first step we discussed a team's two main roles: team leader and team member. There are several other distinct roles and functions that every winning team needs to be successful: sponsor, facilitator, scheduler, and record keeper.

Sponsor

Teams can be formed for different purposes—a short-term project, an effort to solve a problem, or as an ongoing part of the organization. To help a team to be successful in an organization, it may be important to have a sponsor. A sponsor is typically a member of mid-level or senior-level management who oversees the work of the team. That sponsor might also report team progress to a senior management steering committee who oversees a series of improvement processes or other committees. The role of the sponsor includes some or all of these responsibilities:

- establishes the role of the team and helps to draft the team charter
- may select a team leader and team members
- is ultimately responsible for the ongoing efforts and outcomes of the committee
- provides ongoing coaching, resource allocation, and may "run interference" for the team when issues arise with stakeholders or other department staff
- helps the team identify alignment issues with other projects, or with the organization's goals or strategic plan
- serves as an organizational sponsor for the changes that the team ultimately recommends and helps to coordinate integration of these changes in the organization.

Facilitator

Often the facilitator is not a member of the team. The job of the facilitator is to ensure things move smoothly. Facilitators are neutral in nature and use tools such as ground rules, meeting agendas and schedules, parking lots, brainstorming, and prioritizing to assist the team in moving forward. Their job is not to offer advice or opinions or to make decisions, but rather to help the team move forward through a planning or decision-making process. Facilitators are also experts in dealing with difficult people such as a "Negative Nelly" or a "Chatty Chip."

Scheduler

This structured individual is responsible for scheduling meeting locations and activities. She or he sets agendas and puts time constraints into the team's schedule. The scheduler communicates regularly with the team about the next meeting's location and agenda, including topics that require preparation. The scheduler ensures that everyone is aware of what's next.

Record Keeper

This key function requires a team member who possesses an incredible amount of organization. The record keeper updates the team-meeting minutes, takes down lists of ideas, identifies key notes from brainstorming sessions, records significant ideas or tasks, and updates key documents regarding team process and progress.

Enhance Skills and Use Talents

According to best-selling author Marcus Buckingham (2007), you can effectively enhance people's skills and knowledge, but you cannot change a person's innate talents. Realize that people are who they are; you can't change them. However, you can teach them new skills and impart new knowledge. Certain characteristics we have remain the same throughout our lifetimes such as a sense of adventure. Other aspects, such as our value system, change and grow as we do.

As you select team members, consider the end game before you begin. Visualize each member's contribution to the goal looking at his or her specific strengths and weaknesses. Teams provide unique opportunities to teach new skills, increase confidence, and build trust within your organization and your team.

Focus on Strengths

The Gallup organization studied employee engagement and strengths, published in *Strength Finder 2.0* by Tom Rath (2007). Three key findings help us in assessing and engaging team members. If your leader

- primarily ignores you, your chances of being actively disengaged are 40 percent.
- focuses on your weaknesses, your chances of being actively disengaged are 22 percent.
- focuses on your strengths, your chance of being actively disengaged is only 1 percent.

This data suggests that we must focus more on team members' strengths and less on their weaknesses. Although this is easy to say, it's another thing to really do it. Companies, schools, and most personal relationships aren't built on strengths. Typically these relationships are focused on what you must improve. You only have to think of your last annual review, a child's disappointing report card, or an argument with a significant other to realize this is true. The Gallup Organization surveyed over 10 million individuals and discovered only one-third of employees agree they use their strengths daily (Rath 2007). Simply put, we have some work to do. See the pointer on the next page for an idea on how to highlight the strengths of your team members.

POINTER

The freedom to do your own thing ends when you have obligations and responsibilities. If you want to fail yourself—you can—but you cannot do your own thing if you have responsibilities to team members.

—*Lou Holtz*

Sweet Strength Training for Your Team, from Lanie Jordan

Gather several mini candy bars (between three to five for each team member): Kisses, Kudos, Mars Bars, Crunch Bars, Reese's Cups, Snickers, and so on. Place them in several large containers.

Have each team member attach notes to each candy bar such as:

- Kisses—because you love what you do!
- Kudos—you always give credit to others!
- Mars Bars—you have the most creative and out-of-this-world ideas!
- Crunch Bars—you always get projects completed accurately and on time!
- Reese's Bars—your cup runs over with work yet you always stop to help your teammates!
- Snickers—you always make work so much more fun!

Encourage team members to use their imagination and award candy bars to those who have helped them with a problem or whom they've worked with previously.

If your group is struggling to see their own strengths or the strengths of their team members (and your team is small enough), ask that they personally create one note for each team member. If your group is large, draw names so that everyone receives a candy bar.

Possible discussion questions to ask the group after distributing the candy bars: How did you feel when you received your recognition? How did it feel when you recognized someone else? What makes this experience different from having a manager or supervisor recognize you? What would be the response if we gave recognition to the outside sponsors of our team, such as customers, vendors, managers, or other departments? How can we value our unique and individual strengths more?

Determine If the Team Is Working

It is important to note that teams develop and mature over time; each team is unique in its development and personality. A popular model for explaining team development was introduced in Step One (forming, storming, norming, performing, and adjourning, identified by Scholtes, Joiner, & Streibel). Lanie Jordan, team builder and sales trainer, takes a deeper look at each of the team's five developmental stages for red-flag activity as well as indicators that help you determine if the team is working effectively.

Forming is the stage during which team members come together, unite, bond, and are oriented to the team's purpose, mission, and objectives. This can be considered the questioning phase as members ask, Why am I here? What are we doing? How are we going to do this? Little work is accomplished at this stage.

- ◆ **Red flags:** Misunderstood objectives, lack of participation, poor listening, indifference, disorder, low morale, low self-esteem, misunderstanding specific roles on the team are signs that the team is not ready to move to the next stage.
- ☑ **We own this:** Members are engaged, clear on the mission, understand their specific roles on the team, ask questions, take notes, and exhibit a high level of self-esteem.

Storming is the stage when the team begins to work and individuals experience heightened levels of emotion and conflict as members seek out and fight for their desired position within the group dynamic. Personal agendas surface within members as they search out and test the boundaries of their group. At this stage, roles and responsibilities are unclear. This can be viewed by outsiders as a group breakdown; however, it is a necessary and normal step in team development.

- ◆ **Red flags:** Team can't agree, personal agendas surface, biases develop, internal conflicts emerge. Negative emotions such as confrontation, resentment, anger, inconsistency, fear of failure, negative energy, and disrespect of others' points of view can be seen.

☑ **We own this:** The team has documented ground rules, has a system for settling disputes, and is aware of the system. They have a positive energy even when they disagree, and personal motives do not dominate the group.

Norming, here group members' enthusiasm increases as they come together and decide how they will achieve the task at hand. They determine how they will communicate to accomplish their work, accept ground rules, and develop their processes for accomplishing work.

- ◆ **Red flags:** Members question their team members' performance, disrespect others, have unclear objectives, are too forceful, listen poorly, and are disengaged.
- ☑ **We own this:** The team respects one another, collaborates without ego, listens, has clear objectives, and comes together for consensus.

Performing, during this stage members accept each other's strengths and weaknesses. They begin maximizing their strengths, solving issues, and making decisions. It is in this stage that the most work is accomplished. Energy and enthusiasm are high as each team member's self-worth grows within the team dynamic.

- ◆ **Red flags:** The team may suffer from a lack of creativity, poor initiative, inflexibility, closed relationships, arrogance, disregard for others, failure to learn, lack of self-confidence, lack of integrity, poor energy, and decreased production.
- ☑ **We own this:** The team is creative, has high energy, a sense of pride, is cohesive, shows respect for one another, has strong self-esteem, is complimentary of others, and achieves its objectives.

Adjourning, the final stage, conclusion is reached and the group disbands.

- ◆ **Red flags:** Team doesn't assess outcomes, the leader, or its members. There is a lack of reward or public praise for team members and their individual accomplishments; they are unsure that outcomes will be adopted. (For more information about assessments see Step Six.)

☑ **We own this:** Team members have acknowledged the team and team member accomplishments and have created assessments regarding team effectiveness, goal clarity, members, and leaders; they have announced new projects and opportunities to continue the momentum and work of the group.

STEP 2

POINTER

A Thought for Team Members

As your team moves through these stages of development, watch out for red-flag activities. Attempt to resolve these as best you can within the team. If this does not work, be sure to raise your concerns to your team leader.

Based on the stages model introduced in Step One, it becomes evident that setting ground rules is paramount in creating a positive environment for team collaboration. It also shows the importance of setting clear goals, defining the overall mission, and ensuring that individual roles are understood by each team member. This may sound simple, yet most teams fail because they have not followed these principles. If people don't understand the mission or the role that they play on the team, attention span, listening, and participation all suffer, causing a buildup of resentment and anger. These attitudes can spread like a cancer to other members, negatively affecting your outcome.

Strike a Delicate Balance in Leadership

Team leaders must keep the group on task and focused while allowing the team to make its own decisions. Leaders are charged with keeping the team motivated and moving forward to accomplish its task. The best leader may or may not be a supervisor or manager in the group, and the leader should never use a position of power to push an agenda.

Through team development, the leader's role evolves and matures much as the team does. Leaders set the tone by example: start meetings on time, clearly set the ground rules, ensure there is buy-in to the team mission, and show enthusiasm for the team.

Using the same model as we did for team members above, let's examine how the leader's role should change during team development and how leaders should work to avoid the red flags and move into the "we own this" zone.

Prepare for Team Development: Leader Role in Forming Stage

Creating an environment of trust, freedom, and empowerment is essential for team leaders. Teams of firemen and policemen build a bond of trust with one another. Over time and as a result of the level of danger associated with their professions, they know that they have each other's backs when times get tough. Likewise, business teams must come to trust each other and understand their roles in achieving the ultimate goal of the team to share and participate fully. Feeling a sense of power and the ability to change current situations or processes will be instrumental in keeping team synergy moving forward. Team leaders play a key role in setting the stage for this kind of trusting and empowering environment. Tips and resources for how to do this are listed in the Appendixes.

POINTER

Thoughts for Team Leaders

Work on putting your own personal beliefs about individuals or issues aside. You can unconsciously communicate harmful feelings or favoritism to others through your body language and attitude.

Enforce the Ground Rules: Leader Role in Storming Stage

Allow for healthy discussion and even grumbling within the group but do not allow this discussion to overpower the team or its mission. Through breakdown many times comes breakthrough; complaints can bring clarity and understanding to your result as long as it's not dominating the meeting or the team's progress.

Set limits, such as time constraints, in your meeting agendas and in your brainstorming sessions. Everyone needs to feel that he or she is playing by the same set of rules.

Advise and Help Solve Problems: Leader Role in Norming Stage

Foster creativity without judgment. The goal of the leader is to ensure that everyone feels comfortable sharing ideas. Fostering a safe environment ensures everyone's voice is heard and respected.

Facilitate Getting Things Done: Leader Role in Performing Stage

Team leaders must ensure everyone is participating. If you see that someone is not engaged, ask his or her opinion or pose an open-ended question to elicit a response. To help clarify the discussion and identify the next action steps and their owners, summarize meeting outcomes, member contributions, and communicate these to the team.

Assess Members and Reward Accomplishments: Leader Role in Adjourning Stage

Celebrate success by reviewing team performance against the goals and objectives. Gather input on what worked well and what can be improved for the next assignment.

High-Performing Teams

The number-one job of teams is to determine what work needs to be done and to do it. In my experience, teams that are focused and understand this principle are the most successful. Effective teams work through barriers and complexities under tight deadlines and are willing to work with others outside the team to get things done.

Occasionally, a team will not only perform but will really gel. Members respect each other as people as well as parts of the team. This team has the right people and skills; it understands its purpose and is working toward the goals the team has set. All of these things can happen on many teams, but the high-performing teams achieve differently: Team goals supersede individual goals and the individuals look out for each other. The members have an emotional connection to one another. These teams are created from within and cannot be predicted, but they can be nurtured and encouraged. Such teams can serve as powerful forces within their organizations and are well worth the time and resources spent to develop them (Katzenback & Smith 2003).

Make It Happen!

There are many stories of great teams—particularly in the world of sports. The important question we should all ask is, "What did these team members do to build a cohesive unit that works to achieve their peak level of performance?" The first component of our answer has to involve the skilled leader/coach who creates a vision. A successful leader is able to consistently articulate that vision in a way that inspires commitment and an ongoing passion to work together through the daily grind as well as the physical and mental constraints to achieve personal and team greatness. The other obvious component is the members of the team. Each member uses his or her talents to fulfill a role for the good of the team in a way that creates synergy and results.

Bill Russell of the Boston Celtics was the leader of such a team. His team won 11 world championships in 13 years. Bill describes his team by saying: "By design and by talent, (we) were a team of specialists, and like a team of specialists in any field, our performance depended both on individual excellence and on how well we worked together." Bill went on to say that there were times when the game got so intense that he "could feel his play rise to a new level. . . . During those spells, I could almost sense how the next play would develop and where the next shot would be taken." This articulates the essence of a highly functioning team with perfect role clarity.

Create an Environment to Encourage Communication

OVERVIEW

Good communication is based on trust

Understand the factors that affect communication

How to give feedback

Manage conflict effectively

Foster communication

Good communication is as stimulating as black coffee and just as hard to sleep after.

—Anne Morrow Lindbergh

You are on a cross-functional team. The sales people and the information technology people have very different views on what the best solution for this problem is. Sales thinks IT doesn't know about or care about the customer's issues. They want the best solution for the customer, but that solution is going to cost more and take longer. The IT manager has stated the constraints and doesn't want to repeat himself. He feels like no one is listening to his concerns about this solution. He is frustrated and has shut down. The team and its progress are at a standstill.

Scenarios like this are common occurrences. Whose role is it to make sure the right discussions happen, even though they are uncomfortable? Who can help quieter members feel more comfortable in speaking up? Most will look to the team leader to do this, but the reality of the matter is that it is everyone's role to foster good communication on a team. Many times questions and observations from fellow team members can do a lot to lessen a strained conversation and encourage colleagues to speak up. Sometimes the leader needs to facilitate a discussion to make sure people are listening to each other and that the pertinent facts come out.

Build on Trust

Good, clear, and honest communication (quality communication) is one of the main keys to team success. Quality conversation is built on the trust established among team members. If we view the team as a body, trust is its life blood. Communication is analogous to the nervous system—coordinating movements and providing information to make everything work together.

Communication covers lots of ground. It provides the process for understanding whether people on the team have the knowledge, skills, and access to the organization to complete their tasks. It keeps team members up to date on the progress and priorities of the project. Communication provides a way to give and receive feedback and is the mechanism used to disseminate information.

Effective teams understand the importance of good communication and generally develop an entire plan just for communication. Two excellent examples of a communication plan are provided in Appendix B. Be sure to check them out as a solid foundation on which to start building your plan. The focus of this step is not on creating the plan, but on creating an environment that fosters good team communication.

POINTER

For Team Leaders

If you are looking for open communication from your team, be careful what you wish for. Be ready for the frank feedback you may receive.

—*Teri Rounsaville*

Three Truths and a Lie

This is a great game to play to help a group get to know each other and to encourage communication.

◆ Each team member writes down, in a random order, four things about him- or herself—three that are true and one that is a lie.

◆ The leader collects all and reads what is written, one at a time.

◆ The team members try to guess who wrote it and which of the four statements is the lie.

◆ Team members keep track of how many people they guessed correctly and which "fact" is the lie.

Understand the Factors That Affect Communication

There are several factors that need to be considered when creating an environment that fosters open communication. Generational differences, cultural implications, and communication styles affect communication and could provide barriers to open communication if not considered and understood.

Generational Differences

Age and generational influences affect the way people communicate. Baby boomers' view of the world and how to get things done is dramatically differently than GenXers and GenYers (Millennials). Different people have different communication preferences. Find out who would prefer to communicate electronically (via text, instant messaging, or social networking). Be attentive to feedback needs and of expectations of the team members. You may need to have conversations about communication ground rules or etiquette. Discussion of this topic could go into great depth, which is beyond the scope of this book; in brief, however, several key generational differences affect communication:

- **Baby boomers** are often competitive, know how to get things done, and are not always good at sharing knowledge and experience. They typically prefer the phone, email, and face-to-face communication styles.
- **GenXers** are known for being technically savvy and resourceful, tend to be more transient, and may not readily trust corporate environments. Their preferred communication style is instant messaging (IM) or social networking.
- **Millennials (GenYers)** may be resistant to negative feedback. Some companies are finding that this cohort arrives with large expectations—perhaps even a sense of entitlement. Being very technically savvy, their preferred communication style is similar to GenX folks: instantaneous transmission via IM or social networking.

To have clear and honest communication it is critical to be aware of these differences. To help bridge these style and preference gaps, focus on commonalities instead of differences. Acknowledge preferences and be flexible so you can vary the style of communication but focus on the shared team goal and trust in one another.

For ongoing work teams, capturing knowledge is another consideration to keep in mind. In a report published in March 2007 by *Inc.com Magazine*, research indicates that retiring baby boomers are expected to disrupt U.S. companies as they retire. Many businesses are not prepared for the loss of experienced workers that will occur over the next decade.

Teams can lose members to promotion, retirement, and other reasons. If one person holds a significant amount of knowledge that is essential to the team's overall success, devise a plan to share and capture that knowledge and experience.

Teresa Hiatt recommends these steps to help solve this problem:

- ◆ Recognize valuable experience and knowledge in your team members
- ◆ Encourage transfer of the knowledge assets to other team members
- ◆ Create passive workplace methods to capture valuable knowledge and experience
- ◆ Develop a lasting repository of knowledge for future use.

Cultural Differences

More and more, teams are working virtually and contain members from different cultures. Communication in this environment can present a number of challenges. To help avoid cultural issues in communication, use these tips:

- ◆ The leader sets the tone and should repeat the major themes for group understanding. If the leader does this well, team members will also feel comfortable doing it.
- ◆ Be sensitive to the pace of the communication (particularly when the medium uses voice technology—phone, web conference, in-person meetings, and so on).
- ◆ Speak slowly and clearly and avoid jargon.

POINTER

Demonstrate patience and empathy in your communication style. Protect what is said so it does not come back and bite the person who said it. To get true productivity out of the team, people need to feel safe. Careers and futures can be changed dramatically if this is not handled correctly.

—*Mark Spencer*

True Story: Language Issues

I was in a meeting with all Chicago-based folks and one manager from China, David. The VP of sales would ask David a question. He would wait a couple of beats and when David didn't respond, he would move on.

I watched carefully and it seemed that at the moment David was ready to respond, the conversation moved on.

We have to remember, when English is not someone's native language he or she has to hear it in English, translate it to the native tongue, think of the answer, and then translate that to English. This takes time to do. We need to allow time for this process to take place. If possible, providing the questions in advance can help improve this situation.

- ◆ Pay attention to receiving and understanding the information's intent (focus on the message, not the delivery).
- ◆ Create an environment in which all ideas can be heard and understood.
- ◆ Restate or rephrase key points to ensure understanding.
- ◆ Give permission to team members to ask for something to be repeated or to ask the speaker to slow down so everyone can understand.

Communication Style Differences

Communication styles can vary dramatically from one team member to another. Therefore, quality conversations often require a careful and thoughtful balance among differing communication styles. People need to be willing to speak up, even if they aren't comfortable doing so. Conversely, sometimes there are team members who are too comfortable speaking up—even on topics in which they don't have expertise.

Generally in a team situation it is wise to avoid speaking too much. Use the following questions as a quick check to see how you may be coming across in a given meeting or conversation:

- Did you cut someone off to interject your ideas?
- Did you restate your ideas often?
- Can you remember and recite others' opinions when they differed from yours?
- Did you find out why their opinions are different?
- Did you give others equal discussion time?
- Were you critical of others' opinions?
- Were you forceful in speaking your mind, perhaps too forceful?

On the other end of the scale, how do you know if you are communicating too little?

- Did you have an opinion but didn't speak up?
- Were you intimidated by someone in the room and let that affect your ability to state your ideas?
- Did you have an idea that you were uncertain would work so you held it back?
- Did you leave frustrated without speaking up about something?

POINTER

Watch your use of sarcasm! It is difficult enough for people steeped in other cultures and languages to understand without the added complexities of sarcasm. Don't do it. If you catch yourself doing this, stop, and explain your real meaning.

Apologize if you have hurt someone's feelings. Even if it "isn't all your fault," apologize that it happened and own up to your part of it.

- Did you doubt if your ideas have worth?
- Do people see you as a contributing member of the team?

If you find you are doing something "too much" or "too little" continue to watch for it. Ask others with whom you feel comfortable to look for this as well and give you feedback if you do it or even while you are doing it.

Give Constructive Feedback

The ongoing process of team development requires effective communication. Part of team communication is the sharing of periodic assessment of the team's strengths and challenges. This typically is most effectively shared in a team meeting. The purpose of this meeting is to communicate what worked and what improvements are needed so that these lessons can be applied to the team's future successes. A good way to initiate the review process is to distribute a set of questions for each team member to answer prior to the review meeting. If you think that there is anxiety among team members about this information, ask for anonymously written answers before the meeting. Typical questions might include

- What successes have you experienced on this team that you want to see repeated in the future?
- What special contributions were made by team members that surprised you or helped make the team process more enjoyable or successful?

- Was there anything new or different done by team members and what was the result? Any ideas how we could continue or improve on this?
- What do we need to continue to do as a team?
- In your opinion, what didn't work so well? How can this problem be prevented in the future?
- Rate the success of this team in working on this project. Use a scale of one to five with five representing "the best team effort possible" and one representing "we have a lot to work on as a team."

STEP **3**

Review and consolidate all answers deleting any names or specifics that might be inappropriate and share the results with the team members.

Manage Conflict Effectively

Conflict within a group should be looked at as a positive occurrence—it means different views are being shared. Good communication in conflicts includes disagreeing with the idea but not attacking the person who had the idea. Personal attacks go beyond conflict and should not be tolerated.

Before conflict happens, it is helpful for each team member to think about and

Tips for Making Team Feedback Positive

Team feedback can be given in various ways. Sometimes the leader provides feedback to individual team members or to the team at large. Other times, peers give feedback to each other. Regardless of who is giving feedback or whether the feedback is positive or negative, use these tips to make this communication effective:

◆ Give feedback on a timely basis.

◆ Remember, communication is two-way, not top-down. If it is two-way, constructive feedback can be less painful.

◆ Gather input from every person because every role is valued in the process.

◆ Encourage team members to ask for feedback.

◆ Deliver feedback conversationally, not as an attack on any ideas or people.

identify his or her natural reaction to conflict. Some people avoid it at all costs. Some hit it head on—sometimes with too much power. Some want to "win" the argument. Some can converse fairly comfortably through it. Some immediately adopt the other person's view, rather than fighting for their own opinions. Some look for compromise, and some collaborate to find a solution. Discussing these differences and styles and identifying each team member's natural reaction can be helpful in dealing with it later on.

If you are on a team that is a bit shy about speaking up, one way to deal with this is to purposely role play a specific topic that could be controversial. People can see what their own biases are. Learning how to debate diplomatically is a great communication skill to have in business today. Create situations—for example, at early team meetings, monthly sales meetings, annual conferences, or training sessions—to cover and practice the topic of "constructive debate."

Lanie Jordan, a colleague, offers her tried-and-true tips, which might be helpful to your team in resolving conflicts (see pointer on next page).

Foster Communication

Are your team members communicating live (all working from the same location—co-located teams), virtually, or a combination of both? Live or co-located teams can easily meet in person for brainstorming and progress sessions. Virtual groups are enhanced through the use of social media, which has changed the way people communicate and collaborate. (Read more regarding forms and uses of communication tools in Step Eight.) Regardless of the geography of the team and the tools used, the same tips apply to fostering communication on any team.

Communicate Regularly

Managers of teams must have tasks and objectives set on a weekly schedule: What are you going to accomplish this week? This should be placed into an email or template document and used as the basis of regular (weekly) discussions. Those discussions should occur on consistent and scheduled days. This not only sets clear expectations but keeps communication open and sets an atmosphere that the

STEP **3**

Conflict Resolution, Simple as ABC

Acknowledge and Approach

The first step to reaching a resolution is to acknowledge that anger exists. Once acknowledged, it becomes easier to place the emotion of anger aside and begin working toward a solution. As you approach one another, ask yourselves these questions:

- How is this conflict affecting our team, ourselves, and each other?
- Why is this issue important to me? Why is this issue important to the other party?
- What biases do we have toward each other?
- How can we move toward a mutually agreeable solution?

Be Positive

- Send an invitation to communicate by asking, "Can we talk?"
- Create a positive tone by stating, "I'd like to make things better between us."
- Recognize others by affirming, "I recognize this is important to you."
- Validate others by saying, "Thank you for helping me see your perspective."

Create Ground Rules and Choose a Mediator if Necessary

- Agree that only one person speaks at a time.
- No interrupting is allowed.
- Truly listen to the other's point of view.
- Find ways to work together and improve the situation.
- Keep a cool head.
- Agree that if you can't agree you will seek assistance through a neutral third party.

Define Issues That Exist

◆ Take turns explaining your positions.

◆ Use effective listening by taking notes, confirming opinions, clarifying, and using open body language.

◆ Speak in a positive way by not placing blame, talk about the facts, and talk about feelings.

◆ Recognize the needs of others.

Effectively Brainstorm Possible Solutions

◆ Each person contributes ideas that satisfy each other's interests and needs.

◆ Don't criticize ideas.

◆ Be open and think outside the box.

◆ Use positive language: "We could" instead of "You can't."

Find Solutions That Are

◆ Mutually beneficial

◆ Specific in nature

◆ Realistic

◆ Balanced.

Get Proactive and Follow Up

◆ Ensure solutions speak to the key issues for both parties.

◆ Agree to meet and follow up on progress; schedule a specific day and time.

Honor and Help Each Other

◆ Recognize that revisions may be necessary.

◆ Be willing to start the process over again if what you've agreed on isn't working.

◆ Keep in mind that this may be the time to bring in a neutral third party to assist you in resolving differences and gaining resolution.

Do not leave communications or weekly objectives to chance when working as a team—especially when working virtually. To say that we'll just "catch up" each week is a recipe for inaction and eventual team disengagement.

—Don Sandel

manager actually "cares" about what the team member is doing.

Use Email Effectively

Email is a common tool that teams use to communicate. Be aware that this mechanism does not allow for two-way communication. If a dialog is needed, consider other ways to do this (phone call, conference call, in-person meeting, and so on.) When you use email to communicate, follow the Ten Email Commandments offered in the pointer.

Provide Information

Do you ever feel the need to make a presentation to your team? Maybe you need to give updates, explain findings, or discuss recommendations. Regardless of the communication forum used (web conference, in-person meeting, conference call) the tips for making your communication clearer and more successful are the same. If you find you are uncomfortable in this role, here are ways to help you be more successful:

- ◆ **Determine the purpose of the presentation.** Is it to inform, update, get support, persuade?
- ◆ **Make notes.** Create notes of the points you want to make but don't write them out word for word.
- ◆ **Rehearse.** Deliver what you want to say in a mirror until you can say it fluidly, comfortably. It may change once you get there, but have a plan.
- ◆ **Use audiovisuals to support your message.** Practice using tools such as projectors, videos, audio, and so forth in advance.
- ◆ **Choose the right level of detail for the audience.** Have additional details available for back up.

POINTER

Ten Commandments of Email

1. Thou shalt include a clear and specific subject line.
2. Thou shalt edit any quoted text down to the minimum thou needest.
3. Thou shalt read thine own message thrice before thou sendest it.
4. Thou shalt ponder how thy recipient might react to thy message.
5. Thou shalt check thy spelling and thy grammar.
6. Thou shalt not curse, flame, spam, or USE ALL CAPS.
7. Thou shalt not forward any chain letter.
8. Thou shalt not use email for any illegal or unethical purposes.
9. Thou shalt not rely on the privacy of email, especially from work.
10. When in doubt, save thy message overnight and reread it in the light of the dawn.

The Golden Rule of Email

That which thou findest painful to receive, thou shalt not send to others.

STEP **3**

◆ **Be flexible.** The length of the meeting or the key topics to cover may change, and you should be able to change up as well.
◆ **Anticipate your team members' reactions.** Be ready for questions they might ask.

Listen

Actively listening to team members is a key role of the leader. It is important to listen to the words they say, but also to

STEP **3**

"hear" the intent or emotion behind the words. Note what is said and what is left unsaid. Demonstrate active listening by paraphrasing and showing empathy for team members. Encouraging conversation and explanation will help uncover needed information and can help team dynamics.

Make It Happen

Communication affects every aspect of our lives—both personally and professionally. For teams especially, communication is essential. Messages must be communicated accurately, effectively, and efficiently. Relationships among members are negatively affected by harsh feedback or criticism. Such communication can alienate people on a team and cause conflict. Conversely, good honest communication can make people feel safe, valued, loyal, and part of a team.

When conflict does occur within the team, however, it should be viewed as an opportunity. When handled well, it can serve as a unifying force rather than a dividing one. My experience is that not everyone in business has good conflict-management skills, even though these skills are critically needed and well worth the effort to develop. Some people want to avoid conflict at all costs; others seem to seek it. You will likely encounter both types of people on a team. To be an effective communicator you must find a respectful way to manage conflict while considering everyone's communication style and feelings.

NOTES:

_____

_____

_____

_____

_____

_____

_____

_____

_____

_____

_____

_____

_____

_____

_____

_____

_____

_____

_____

_____

_____

_____

Build Strong and Effective Relationships

Trust takes time to build but can be dismantled in an instant. It is the most precious commodity in human relations.

—Jerry Acuff

STEP 4

I was once on a board of directors for a national training organization. One member was quite difficult to work with. He appeared very kind and friendly, but his tactics were often underhanded and he had a habit of offending people. Bottom line: He didn't inspire trust in his relationships. Once on a board meeting conference call he made a suggestion for a policy change. I remember arguing against it. His suggestion didn't get enough support to pass. Later on, when reflecting about it, I remember thinking the idea had merit. Ultimately, I believe that if someone with better relationships on the team had introduced the idea, the discussion and outcome would have gone much differently.

Teams are made up of people. Getting to know team members and developing a relationship with them will contribute to the effectiveness of the team. It can also contribute to the motivation of the team members.

Having a valuable business relationship with members of any team that you are on is crucial. Teams work best when there is role clarity, goal clarity, and trust. Nothing contributes to this more than a great business relationship with your other team members. The investment we make in building these relationships is one of the wisest investments we can make in ourselves and in our success.

—*Jerry Acuff,*
The Relationship Edge in Business

STEP 4

Build Strong Relationships

One of the most important things you can bring to a team is the ability to develop and sustain good relationships. Good people skills are vitally important to a team's success. Strong relationships among team members also help minimize the need for conflict resolution. One team member can have the perfect solution to a problem, but if she or he has alienated the team members, these ideas may not be adopted or taken seriously.

Strong leadership on this issue is very important, but there are also many areas that team members themselves can work on to help foster cohesion and build relationships among team members:

- ◆ **Establish ongoing communication.** Begin with clear communication about work expectations and continue to communicate often throughout the team project. This helps keep everyone on the same page and helps the team get to know each other better as individuals.
- ◆ **Cultivate openness**. Sharing information about yourself, exhibiting vulnerability, and being totally open and up front will help foster a sense of openness within the team.

Use one or both suggestions to facilitate team sharing and help build stronger relationships within the team.

◆ At the first meeting, ask the team leader to answer the following question: "If you really knew me you would know . . . " At each subsequent meeting ask for volunteers to offer response to the same question.

◆ Have team members create a PowerPoint slide with pictures of themselves and indicate interests and things that are important to them. Share the slides at in-person meetings or via webcast so people can get to know each other.

STEP **4**

◆ **Encourage social interaction**. Look for a variety of opportunities for the team to interact on a social basis. Lunches, breaks, and after-work activities serve as good opportunities for group members to get to know more about each other socially and professionally.

◆ **Share nonwork information**. Successful teams set aside time for team members to visit with each other. Team meetings often include a bit of time for members to talk about things important to them outside of their work.

◆ **Embrace respect**. It is crucial to create a value system that embraces and respects differences among team members so strong relationships can be built. Be sure to create a team mission statement that includes the word "respect."

◆ **Work toward mutual trust**. As people begin to trust each other they will be more likely to communicate risks and reveal difficult milestones and deadlines. Mutual trust is crucial for effective relationship building.

Meet Challenges to Building Relationships Head On

There are several aspects of teams in general and of team members in particular that can get in the way of building strong relationships, if you let them. The key is to be aware of these challenges before they begin and to work on strategies to avoid any roadblocks.

Cross-Generational Teams

World events, technological advances, and popular culture all shape the values and perspectives of different generations. You may find many baby boomers to be very relational. It is a significant way they get things done. You may find that younger folks in the workforce do not share that same mentality. They may think boomers are inflexible to change. Older workers may find boomers to be too open and younger audiences unwilling to share as much. These workers may feel that the texting and instant messaging technologies get in the way of building relationships.

What is the generational lesson for building relationships? By focusing on the values that different generations bring to the overall strength of the team, team members can learn from each other. More mature team members may contribute a historical perspective to younger generations, whereas younger generations may keep the team up to date on technology and media. To prevent intergenerational conflict that can hinder relationship development, common values among team members, such as family, work/life balance, and achievement, should be highlighted. And of course, reminding everyone of the unifying goal of the team helps keep things on track.

Cross-Functional Teams

There are often people outside of the team whose expertise or assistance are important to the team's success. Building relationships across the whole organization adds a new dimension to building relationships among team members. If it is an all-sales team, people will likely know each other or know of each other. When a team is made up of people who don't know each other—and don't even know what others do—it is particularly important to provide opportunities for people to get to know each other early on. These opportunities will help break down any "silent" barriers while building camaraderie.

How does one build cross-functional teams? Consider ways for each team member to get to know and understand the skills of others who have different functions. Ask questions about what these people do for the company. Work to find out how they fit into the team. Another aspect of this type of team is to understand the rules of engagement for using resources from differing areas within the organization. With cross-functional teams it is essential to set clear expectations so that role assumptions do not jeopardize relationships.

Across-the-Globe Teams

Geography can present another potential challenge to building relationships. Sometimes it's hard enough to build a relationship with someone who is on another floor in your building, let alone on another continent. As geographically dispersed and virtual teams become more prevalent, the technology to support these teams improves, as does our learning and experience with these challenges.

This real-life scenario shared by my colleague Amy Tupler explains some of the challenges of geographically dispersed teams and shows one way that a team solved this problem:

> I worked on several global teams and there are a few tips that worked well. One big change that improved relationships was to shift the quarterly meeting time so

POINTER

For Team Members

Particularly early on, when you are building your relationships and your credibility, keep your promises, meet your deadlines, and do what you say you will do. If you know you cannot make an assigned deadline, ask for help. By nurturing your team relationships, you need to be honest with yourself and your team members. Once you have a relationship and credibility is established a missed deadline or missed follow-through can often be taken in stride.

that non-U.S.-based teams felt as important as the head-quarters team members. At Motorola, the entire world revolved around Chicago, which was annoying for the non-Illinois-based groups. [To address this issue], the Florida team members would drive the meeting times for the call in Q1. Then in Q2, it might be Singapore. In Q3, it might be China and in Q4, it would be India. This way, everyone was inconvenienced (late night or early morning) equally (sort of) and given the opportunity to "drive" the call in their style.

What is the lesson for building geographically dispersed teams? Fostering strong relationships among team members early in the game is critical. Give all locations a chance to lead or "drive." Schedule face-to-face meetings if possible to kick off the project, and help the team get to know each other. If meeting in person is not an option, leverage technology to enable communication, foster interaction, and share information—both of a nonbusiness and professional nature. (For more information about these technologies and tips about working virtually, see Step Eight.)

Establish a Process for Building Team Relationships

Building relationships is a skill that needs to be nurtured. Jerry Acuff, in *The Relationship Edge in Business*, offers a three-step process for building relationships (2004):

- **Step 1: Have the right mindset.** To cultivate this you must value relationships as important, believe that others will want a relationship with you, and be willing to see things from another's perspective.
- **Step 2: Ask the right questions.** It is necessary to ask good questions in the right way and for the right reasons. You are looking for things you have in common with the others. Or, you might find out something about a topic you didn't know before.
- **Step 3: Take the right actions.** Show consideration by remembering special events and treating people consistently well. Be sincere and show that you really do care. And, finally, listen, listen, listen.

When team members make it a priority to get to know each other, and the team leader creates opportunities for this to happen, relationships can grow and business results can be dramatic.

POINTER

For Team Leaders

A team leader who is open and accessible is a key driver of building trust. Although some things need to be confidential, share as much as possible with team members. Scheduling informal meetings, gatherings, or conversations to get to know each other will set a climate for trust. As team members meet their commitments and follow through, people will begin to realize who they can rely on.

STEP 4

Find Common Ground

Getting to know people is like peeling an onion. Initially you experience the surface layer. As you get to know your teammates you begin peeling back the layers. Getting to know them on a deeper level helps you develop more of a bond and fosters mutual respect and trust. But how do you do this? One way is by finding things you have in common. Have you ever noticed that when you have something in common with someone—you are from the same city, have the same alma mater, both play golf, both have dogs, have young kids or teenagers—conversation comes easily? It is much easier to get comfortable with someone and have easy dialogue when you have things in common. So, one way to start developing relationships is to find something you have in common. How can you find common ground? Ask great questions!

So, when asking questions to find something in common with someone, do you sit down and interrogate the person with a list of questions all at once? Not if you are trying to connect in a positive way. Think about it and plan ahead. Start with what you know and then move on to what you can ask to find out. Jerry Acuff says the way you ask the question is as important as the question itself. He suggests prefacing the question with something like, "Since we will be working together on this project for awhile, I would love to know more about you. Do you mind if I ask . . . " Or, "It occurs to me that even though we have worked together, I don't know a lot about what is important to you . . . " The way you set up the question can help put the other person at ease.

Email is sometimes an inhibitor to finding common ground and building initial relationships. It is much more common to ask people-connection questions on the phone or in person. These mediums are better for holding conversations in which to pose questions and give responses. If you find yourself using email in the first stages of forming team relationships, make sure your emails are not "sterile." Start with a salutation. Add a personal touch, even if it is brief.

Ask these initial questions to get the conversation going and to help find common ground:

Family

◆ Do you have siblings, kids?
◆ What are your kids' ages and interests?
◆ Where did you grow up?
◆ Do you have pets?

Occupation

◆ How did you get into your field?
◆ What do you find interesting or challenging in your job?
◆ What are your career aspirations?
◆ What is you educational background?

Recreation

◆ What do you do for fun?
◆ Do you like sports/music/arts/theater?
◆ Do you belong to a club or charitable group?
◆ What do you do on vacation?
◆ Do you like books/movies?
◆ Do you like travel?
◆ What hobbies do you have?

Motivation

◆ What are your dreams or wishes?
◆ What gets you out of bed in the morning?
◆ What do you aspire to?
◆ What inspires you?

STEP 4

A Real-Life Example

An English co-worker once made the following comment to a peer from Chicago: "In your emails you just tell us what you want us to do. You don't say hello. You don't ask how we are." The two had been working together for almost a year by the time she mentioned this. She, and others on the British team, had noticed this about their U.S. co-workers and had discussed it among themselves, but she waited until they were face to face to mention it to her American colleague.

The lesson here is that if your primary method of contact is email, take an additional step to make the communication relational. If these behaviors don't come naturally to you, you will have to be very conscious and deliberate about being conversational. After awhile, unconsciously your style will change and you will write more conversationally. It will just be part of what you do and how you relate in email. It's important to remember that not everyone will cooperate and want a good relationship with you. All you can do is try.

So far we have reviewed some ideas on how to get to know people on your team. Worksheet 4-1 offers a tool that may help you to determine where your relationships are strong and where you need to focus your efforts. You will find the people you do not have a natural connection with (or common ground) will be harder to get to know. Think about which people these are and develop a plan to build stronger relationships.

Make It Happen

By their nature, teams thrive on strong interpersonal relationships. It is the synergy created by relationships and a sense of community that make teams effective.

Some people connect with others naturally and, for them, building strong relationships is easy. For others it is not natural, and focus and work will be needed to build relationships. No matter where your natural tendencies lie, know that it is important to develop relationships with people you are working with. On teams,

Tips for Building Relationships

Team Leaders

- Be available, be social.
- Show interest in your team members; find out what is important to them.
- Demonstrate respect for all people and ideas, even if they disagree with your thoughts.
- Say "please" and "thank you."
- Ask for advice.
- Connect with people who are not outspoken and help increase their comfort. Help them to articulate their ideas.
- Praise contributions.
- Demonstrate good listening skills and ask questions for clarification.
- Collaborate and encourage collaboration.

Team Members

Develop a relationship with the team leader:

- Find out how and when to send updates.
- What does the leader want to know about and what does he or she want you to handle?
- What is the right detail level?
- What are his or her dreams for the team?
- How does the leader define success?

Develop relationships with team members:

- Do what you said you were going to do.
- Be open to feedback, avoid being defensive.
- Communicate directly and be respectful.
- Give updates on your progress.
- Demonstrate your commitment to the team.
- Be a good and supportive team member.
- Don't feel the need to hog all the credit.

WORKSHEET 4.1
How Strong Are Your Relationships?

Use this worksheet to enhance the relationships you have and determine those you need to build to be successful on your team. Assess the team—Who do you know, how do you know them? Now, determine how well you know everyone on a scale of 1 to 5. One means that you recognize them by sight, five means that you have established a good relationship with them over a period of time.

Who?   **How well? (1–5)**

_____

_____

_____

_____

_____

_____

Who do you need to get to know, and how will you do that? Include those from the list above who are ranked 1, 2, or 3.

Who?   **How?**

_____

_____

_____

_____

_____

_____

_____

Assess your network outside of the team. Who do you need to know? How will you get to know them?

Who?   **How?**

_____

_____

_____

_____

_____

_____

_____

Assess your relationship with the team leader, stakeholder, and sponsor. Who do you need to get to know?

Who?   **How?**

_____

_____

_____

_____

_____

_____

_____

STEP **4**

people rely on each other. A personal relationship can make the difference between a team that feels like work and drudgery and a team that people look forward to participating on.

STEP **4**

NOTES:

_____

_____

_____

_____

_____

_____

_____

_____

_____

_____

_____

_____

_____

_____

_____

_____

_____

_____

_____

_____

_____

_____

_____

Build Processes to Track Progress and Get Things Done

The importance of process

Identify and implement team processes

Track results

Provide updates

Deal with problems

If you want predictable results, follow the recipe.

—Renie Francke

Along with being a fabulous person, my Aunt Renie was the consummate baker. She made amazing desserts. Every time she set out to bake, she pulled out one of her many recipe books. She had made these recipes, successfully, hundreds of times and knew most by heart. Even so, she still looked up the recipe. When I asked her if she ever just winged it, she said, "If you want predictable results, follow the recipe."

The Importance of Process

Just as my Aunt Renie taught me, there is a relationship between using a well-tested recipe and reaping the reward of delicious cookies. I have learned too that there is a relationship between following a process and having a team achieve its desired outcome. Successful teams use repeatable processes that they apply over and

Team members build trust in one another by overcoming challenges together and winning! Successful teams need to be flexible, truly collaborative, have some overlap between members for purposes of redundancy and contingencies (illness, resignation, etc.). Good teams are somewhat self-policing in terms of staying on task.

—*Cary Dudczak*

over. These teams also know when something is not working and have a process to change and improve their performance. Following defined processes delivers results and provides a framework in which to track results and progress.

Teams, at least initially, consist of individuals with different backgrounds and experiences. Research shows that it is not just a nicety for team members to get along together—it's a necessity. Successful teams are about leveraging the skills and experiences of others and challenging team members to change their behavior to accommodate the needs of the team, rather than their own needs. Therefore, teaching the individuals on a team—from the very start—how to work well together is critical to the team's long-term success.

One of the keys to success when using processes is having just the right amount of choice. Remember the story about Goldilocks and the chairs? The first one was too hard, the next one was too soft, the third one was just right. (If this children's story doesn't ring a bell, take a quick look at *Goldilocks and The Three Bears*.) Processes that are too cumbersome will get in the way. Too much effort will be spent on the process, which will get in the way of achieving results. Too few processes can mean duplication of work or steps being omitted, which can negatively affect quality and cause rework. When a variety of people are doing different parts of the work or project, the "just right" process can help streamline the effort and make sure everything gets done as planned.

Productive teams can be built by establishing standard processes that team members agree to follow. Standard processes give everyone on the team a common framework to work from, regardless of their varied experiences and past work styles. Processes define what *this* team experience will be, and how *this* team will function.

Identify and Implement Team Processes

Chances are good that your organization has existing processes in place for many aspects of your team's work. Most likely there are organizational processes, project processes, and general team processes. Start with those that have worked in the past and make sense for your team. Modify them as needed by adding or removing elements for your team. Below are a few examples of some of the kinds of processes that may be helpful for your team.

Onboarding

The makeup of teams is bound to change over the duration of the team charter. Having a process to quickly and efficiently bring new players onboard will

POINTER

There are some who would argue that following the same process over and over leaves little room for innovation or creativity, but this is not so! Just as you can "spice up" a cookie recipe with your own "secret ingredient," the same can be done with standard processes. When creating or adapting a process, be sure to get the basics down first, and then add the team's flair or signature. Make improvements as needed.

STEP **5**

help keep the momentum going and
get them up to speed quickly. Table
5.1 presents a sample checklist to use
when bringing on new team members.

Communication

Successful teams are expert at communicating with each other. (For more
about establishing and encouraging effective team communication, refer to
Step Three.) How will your team communicate? Much depends on the location of your team and each person's
role on it. In general, it's a good practice to establish a firm game plan for
communication. High-functioning
teams have a developed plan that speci-
fies the process of what needs to be
communicated, who is to communicate
it, the frequency of the communication, and the method to be used for
the communication.

A good sample of a communication
process and plan is found in Appendix
B (see Sample Communication Plan)
and is available for download from
www.astd.org/10steps2teams. This example provides an overall plan of the
weekly communications for the
project.

TABLE 5.1

Sample Onboarding Checklist

New Team Member Checklist	Things to Include	Status
Give Access to Team Resources *Be sure to consider both electronic and paper-based information.*	Information access • Access paths, user ID, passwords, etc. for team servers, data, other systems Physical access • To buildings, offices, parking, etc. • Keys, badges, vehicle stickers, access codes, etc. • Other _____	
Distribute a Team Chart *Be sure to include your new team member's information on the Team List.*	Team list • Role, contact info, photo, and other info • Other _____	
Provide the Team Background	Team documentation • Charter • Rules • Processes • Project Plan Other documents: • _____ • _____ • _____ • _____	
Introduce to Team Members	Introduce new team member (can be done at a status meeting, informally, or during a teleconference)	
Schedule of Ongoing Meetings	Established dates and meetings • Team calendar • Scheduled meetings • Project timeline • Other _____	
Other		

STEP **5**

Problem Resolution

Teams often find the need for a problem-resolution process. Typically each organization has some general guidelines and steps (process) for working through problems. This process usually includes procedures to escalate an issue if it cannot be resolved through the problem-resolution process. Step Nine also offers other insights and tips for problem solving in team situations.

Track Results

Once the core processes are in place and things are starting to get done, it's important to be able to see where you are in the process. Teams need to be able to figure out what has been completed and what remains to be done. This is another type of process—tracking results. The kind of results your team needs to track depend on your goals and objectives. Examples of the kinds of things a team might want to track include

- project milestones
- tasks to be completed, by whom, and by when
- overall team progress as compared to goals
- financial data (costs, revenue, sales, and so forth)
- quality
- customer satisfaction.

Provide Updates

Providing updates on team progress is a process that is closely linked to tracking. The team will need to develop a method for supplying these updates. Sometimes this type of information is included in the communication plan. Other times, updates are part of tracking results and occur when project milestones are reached. Updates that may need to be supplied include

- updating stakeholders
- updating team leader or project sponsors
- milestone updates to team members.

When giving updates, even though it may be difficult, be complete. Do not shy away from or leave out any risks or bad news. It's much better to prepare people for what might happen—good or bad. No one wants to be surprised with bad news. Indicating potential hazards or risks before they occur can help elevate the issue and stimulate action to avoid these possible obstacles.

Deal with Problems

Sometimes a process works at the beginning of a project but then ceases to be effective. What can cause a process to stop working or become less effective? Listen for some of the common symptoms listed in Table 5.2, which may indicate there is a problem with your team process.

If existing processes don't work for your team, it may be time to create something new. When creating new processes, be sure to take into account the type of activity for which you are creating the process. How detailed or complex is it? Is a process for this action really needed? Sometimes a list of bullet points works well. Other times, very detailed steps are required. For processes in which there are many steps or several processes are involved, consider creating a flow chart or other visual representation of the steps involved. Sometimes a picture is worth a

POINTER

If your stakeholders don't know what you're doing, they'll assume you're doing nothing. If they assume you're doing nothing, one of two things will happen: You'll have even more to do, or you'll have nothing to do.

—*Terrence Donahue*

TABLE 5.2

Common Symptoms of Managing versus Leading

Symptom	Problem	Action
"We didn't plan for *that* to happen . . . " "*That's* never happened before."	Poor or incomplete design	When adopting, adapting, or creating processes, try to consider all possibilities no matter how remote.
"I didn't think it was important to . . . " "Does the order of the steps really matter?"	Poor execution of the process; didn't follow process correctly	Review the processes as a team early on. Be sure to share the processes with members who join the team later.
"I thought I was supposed to . . . " "*Whose* role is it to . . . "	Lack of understanding or communication; roles or transition points not clear	Make sure all parties involved are clear about their roles and that the hand-off is explained.
"I never knew we had a process for . . . " "No one ever does that . . . "	Process ignored or never presented	Review the processes as a team early on or as part of a later team meeting if needed. Remember to share the processes with members who join the team later.

thousand words in helping to convey the way a process works. See Figure 5.1 for an example of a visual process.

Make It Happen!

While working on various project teams, many years after first learning about baking, I was able to equate what I learned in my aunt's kitchen to my job. If you want consistent results and the

FIGURE 5.1

Visual Process Example

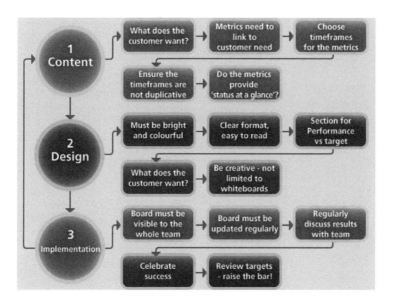

ability to deliver expected outcomes, processes must be followed. I also learned that team processes, like recipes, often require steps done in a specific sequence, with inputs added in set amounts and at specified times. If you deviate too far from the process, add things out of order, or do things outside of the established timeframes, you can wind up with a flop.

Keep in mind that it takes time and patience to develop an effective process. When it is right, you can just taste it—much like Aunt Renie's cookies. Don't be afraid to try a new recipe and don't be afraid to fail. Each failure brings you that much closer to success! When you do have a recipe that provides success, don't be afraid to experiment by adding or changing ingredients—you could get even better results! A good recipe for effective teams includes members who work at making the processes succeed for their group and their goals.

NOTES:

Assess the Team Regularly for Top Performance

The person who gets the farthest is generally the one who is willing to do and dare. The sure-thing boat never gets far from shore.

—Dale Carnegie

STEP 6

Have you ever had a performance appraisal and been surprised by the results? For most of us, the answer probably is "yes." Instead of giving you immediate feedback, your manager saved it up and delivered it to you in your year-end performance review—when it was too late to do anything about it. Don't you wish you would have gotten feedback earlier, so you could have corrected the situation right away? Conducting an assessment is a way for team leaders and team members to get immediate feedback on what they're doing well and which areas need development. It's best to assess early on—before the team gets to the end of a project when it's too late to do anything differently.

Why Use Assessments?

After a team is formed, a particularly useful exercise to foster team building is to have the team determine its strengths and development needs. One possible exception for this recommendation might be if the leader knows all the team members well and the team members know each other well. However, even in this circumstance, assessments still can be helpful. After all, to improve anything, you first need to know what's working and what's not. Conducting an assessment provides this information. Assessment results offer greater clarity of team member roles, responsibilities, and expectations.

There are two team assessments contained in this step. One is designed specifically for team leaders and the other for team members. Both consist of 36 statements divided into nine scales or dimensions. The dimensions have been identified through behavioral science research as being critical to the effective functioning of a team (Biech 2001). However, all nine dimensions may not be equally important to the functioning of your particular team. In fact, a useful team-building exercise is to take the nine dimensions and have a team discussion regarding the importance each dimension should play in defining how the team functions. Here is a brief description of each of the nine dimensions:

- **Open and clear communication**—assesses extent to which team leaders and team members establish a communicative atmosphere during team discussions that is marked by openness, honesty, respect for others, and two-way interactions.
- **Problem solving and decision making**—assesses extent to which team leaders and team members engage in team problem solving and decision making using a systematic, participative, and actionable approach.
- **Cooperative relationships**—assesses extent to which team leaders and team members strive to create a team atmosphere characterized as supportive, inclusive, and respectful.

- **Goal oriented**—assesses extent to which team leaders and team members contribute to a sense of team goal attainment.
- **Trust**—assesses extent to which team leaders and team members strive to build a team atmosphere of mutual trust among all team members.
- **Relationship with management/team leader**—assesses extent to which team leaders keep management informed about important team issues and team members do the same with team leaders.
- **Accountability**—assesses extent to which team leaders and team members strive to build an atmosphere of personal accountability in which team members keep commitments, face up to mistakes, and regularly give and receive performance feedback.
- **Cross-cultural sensitivity**—assesses extent to which team leaders and team members recognize the value of team member differences and find ways to leverage these when performing team tasks.
- **Managing conflict**—assesses extent to which team leaders and team members strive to constructively overcome conflict in a way that is satisfactory to both parties.

STEP **6**

Team Leader Assessment

The Team Leader Self-Assessment is designed to help team leaders identify their strengths and development needs to effectively lead the team. For new team leaders, this insight will help shorten the transition time needed to become a fully functioning team leader. Experienced team leaders, in contrast, are likely to already have a general sense of what they do well and what development needs they have, but they may be unaware of the specifics. Although having a general idea of one's strengths and development needs is good, knowing the specifics is even better. It is only by knowing the specifics that a team leader can identify definite action steps to take to improve his or her skills. The Team Leader Self-Assessment (Worksheet 6.1) is found at the end of this step and available for download at www.astd.org/10steps2teams.

Team Member Assessment

For Team Leaders

Use the nine dimensions as a team-building exercise. Engage your team in a discussion concerning the importance each dimension should play in defining how the team functions.

To maximize their potential and effectiveness, teams not only need skilled leaders but also team members who take responsibility for how the team operates and who possess specific skills that aid the team in accomplishing its tasks. It's not enough merely to be a team member. The Team Member Self-Assessment (Worksheet 6.2) provided in this step is designed to help team members identify their strengths and development needs to increase their effectiveness. This tool is designed along the same lines as the Team Leader Self-Assessment but takes a different perspective. The Team Member Self-Assessment has a variety of potential uses:

◆ **Forming a new team**—When a team is first formed, the assessment can be used to raise important issues to talk about as a team. Included among these are establishing ground rules for how the team will function, identifying communication norms and problem-solving approaches, and so on. Getting these types of things out in the open when a team is first forming can prevent problems later.

◆ **Re-energizing a plateaued team**—Sometimes teams stall out or get in a rut and need a boost to get back on track. The assessment can be used to identify specific areas that are presenting difficulty for the team. Once identified, a plan can be developed to overcome these and get the team back on track.

◆ **Keeping an experienced team on track**—Even experienced, fully functioning teams may need an occasional "shot in the arm" to stay on track. When everything is working well, it's easy to get complacent or to fall into bad habits and not even be aware that things have gotten off track. Periodically completing the assessment is a way for teams to identify areas in which complacency or bad habits may have made an inroad so that they can be dealt with by the team.

Periodically completing the assessment is also a good way to remind every one on the team about what is important.

Tips for Using Assessments

You can use these assessments in a variety of ways. Here are three suggestions for their use on your team.

Complete and Meet

One approach is to have everyone on the team complete the Team Member Self-Assessment and then use the Your Skill Scores section of this worksheet to determine the scores for each of the nine dimensions. Then, the members will use Worksheet 6.3 (Analyzing Your Scores) to help determine their own individual action plans. (These documents are found at the end of this step, as well as available for download at www.astd.org/10steps2teams.) Reproduce the appropriate pages and distribute a set to each team member or give a book to each team member. After all team members have completed the assessment, set aside a segment of time during a team meeting to discuss these questions: What was learned? What surprises were there, if any? What should the team be doing differently?

POINTER

For Team Members

Once you have identified a development need, it's important to craft a plan for improvement. Use your imagination and be creative when looking for resources and education on the topics. Consider resources both within and outside your organization.

STEP **6**

Team Roll-Up

A second approach is to have all team members complete the assessment and turn their scores in to the team leader. The team leader can then aggregate the individual team member scores to calculate an overall team score. Again, set aside some time during a team meeting to discuss the results and answer the questions posed earlier.

Pair and Share

A third approach is to have all team members complete the assessment and then, during a team meeting, pair up and share their scores. After a few minutes, the team leader can then engage the team in a discussion using the three questions listed.

Ken Phillips (performance management and sales performance consultant who developed these assessments) emphasizes that both assessments are intended for development purposes only. They should not be used simply to evaluate a team leader or team member.

Make It Happen!

Everyone loves to take quizzes to find out more about him- or herself. Think of this as another opportunity to find out more about yourself and about your team members. A tip for everyone: Be open and honest when you take these assessments. Even if all of your scores are relatively high, look at the lowest score as an area you can improve. Take advantage of every development opportunity that comes your way. It will help the team as well as you.

WORKSHEET 6.1
Team Leader Self-Assessment

Note

Please keep in mind that the results from this inventory will be helpful to you only to the extent that they are an accurate reflection of your actual team leader behavior. Therefore, it is to your benefit to respond as candidly as possible.

Instructions

- The inventory consists of 36 statements which describe a team leader's behavior with his or her team members.

- Carefully read the first statement. Keeping in mind your own approach to leading a team, indicate how often you engage in the behavior along a continuum from *Never* to *Always*.

- Place an X in the circle that corresponds to your choice for each statement. Place an X in only one circle per statement. You must make a choice for all 36 statements in order for the assessment to be scored accurately.

- Make your choices based on how you actually behave, not on how you think you should behave.

Developed by Kenneth R. Phillips, Founder and President, Phillips Associates, Grayslake, Illinois.

(continued on next page)

STEP 6

		NEVER				ALWAYS
1.	During team discussions, I like to have both myself and the other team member(s) take charge.	①	②	③	④	⑤
2.	I strive to develop group cohesiveness.	①	②	③	④	⑤
3.	I strive to create an atmosphere where team members respect one another and enjoy working together.	①	②	③	④	⑤
4.	I establish specific, measurable team goals and ensure that each team member understands the reasons for having the goals.	①	②	③	④	⑤
5.	I make an effort to get to know all the members of my team as individuals and not just team members.	①	②	③	④	⑤
6.	I make a point to inform my manager and other company executives about what is happening with the team and any successes we've had.	①	②	③	④	⑤
7.	I strive to create an atmosphere where team members keep commitments and consistently do what they agree to.	①	②	③	④	⑤
8.	I recognize that diversity in thoughts and culture strengthen the team and I look for ways to take advantage of these during team meetings and discussions.	①	②	③	④	⑤
9.	When differences arise during team meetings, I try to get the opposing team members to understand and state the points of view of the other.	①	②	③	④	⑤
10.	I strive to create an atmosphere of open, two-way communication between myself and the other team members.	①	②	③	④	⑤

STEP 6

		NEVER				ALWAYS
11.	When a problem is identified, I share equally with the team in solving it.	①	②	③	④	⑤
12.	I strive to create an atmosphere where team members recognize and praise each other for their specific accomplishments.	①	②	③	④	⑤
13.	I include team members in the setting of team goals and milestones in order to create a feeling of commitment and ownership.	①	②	③	④	⑤
14.	I strive to develop a positive and supportive relationship with each member of the team.	①	②	③	④	⑤
15.	When team accomplishments are recognized by upper management, I make sure the entire team is recognized and not just selected individuals.	①	②	③	④	⑤
16.	I provide regular feedback to each team member to reinforce things they've done well and correct things that need improvement.	①	②	③	④	⑤
17.	During team discussions, I make sure every team member has an opportunity to state his or her point of view and have it listened to and considered, even if it differs from the norm.	①	②	③	④	⑤
18.	When differences arise during team meetings, I try to keep communication open, candid, and unguarded between the opposing team members.	①	②	③	④	⑤

(continued on next page)

STEP **6**

19.	During team discussions, I ensure that team member ideas are respected and listened to without interruption.	① ② ③ ④ ⑤
20.	When solving problems, I encourage the team to use a systematic, no-blame approach to problem solving and decision-making.	① ② ③ ④ ⑤
21.	I strive to create an atmosphere where team members recognize that they need one another's knowledge, skills, and abilities to successfully complete team tasks.	① ② ③ ④ ⑤
22.	I formally and informally demonstrate a strong professional commitment to achieving our team goals.	① ② ③ ④ ⑤
23.	I make it known that I'm available to help if any team members encounter difficulties accomplishing a task.	① ② ③ ④ ⑤
24.	I keep my manager informed on the status of team projects and what additional resources (time, money, equipment, support), if any, are needed to complete the projects.	① ② ③ ④ ⑤
25.	I provide regular feedback to each team member to ensure that they understand what standards of behavior and performance are and are not acceptable.	① ② ③ ④ ⑤
26.	If any team members make remarks or jokes that could be perceived as derogatory or offensive, I intervene and point out that such behavior is unacceptable.	① ② ③ ④ ⑤

STEP 6

27.	When differences arise during team discussions, I strive to help the opposing team members discover and state explicitly the common interest and goals that they share.	①	②	③	④	⑤
28.	During team discussions, I acknowledge each team member's point of view and ask questions to get more information.	①	②	③	④	⑤
29.	I strive to create a team atmosphere where timely decision-making without procrastination and an appropriate bias toward action are the norm.	①	②	③	④	⑤
30.	I strive to create an atmosphere where team members are helpful and supportive of one another.	①	②	③	④	⑤
31.	I encourage all team members to feel proud each time the team achieves one of its goals.	①	②	③	④	⑤
32.	I keep my promises and respond promptly and willingly to team member requests.	①	②	③	④	⑤
33.	I am sensitive to the many pressures faced by upper management and use this perspective to try and help my team understand why management makes some of the decisions they do.	①	②	③	④	⑤
34.	I strive to create an atmosphere where team members willingly face up to their mistakes and accept responsibility for what happened.	①	②	③	④	⑤

(continued on next page)

STEP
6

		NEVER				ALWAYS
35.	During team meetings, I stress the importance of valuing team member differences and how these are important to team success.	①	②	③	④	⑤
36.	During discussions of differences, I try to get the opposing team members to focus on joint problem solving and identify solutions that are satisfactory to both parties.	①	②	③	④	⑤

STEP **6**

WORKSHEET 6.1

Your Skill Scores

Instructions

- Listed below are the nine dimensions associated with being an effective team member. Numbers to the right represent statements from the assessment. Refer back to statement number one and in the box labeled "1" below, enter the numerical value of the response you chose for that statement. For example, let's say that for statement one you marked a "3." In this case, you would enter 3 in the box labeled "1" below.
- Total the numerical values on each dimension to obtain your skill effectiveness scores.
- After finding your skill effectiveness scores on each dimension, total your scores to determine your Overall Effectiveness.

Dimensions	Statements				Skill Effectiveness
Opening and Clear Communication	1 ☑ +3 ☐	10	19 ☐	28 ☐ = ☐	16
Problem Solving and Decision-Making	2 ☑ +	11 ☐	20 ☐	29 ☐ = ☐	17
Cooperative Relationships	3 ☑ +	12 ☐	21 ☐	30 ☐ = ☐	16
Goal Oriented	4 ☑ +	13 ☑	22 ☐	31 ☐ = ☐	17
Trust	5 ☑ +	14 ☑	23 ☐	32 ☐ = ☐	19
Relationship With Management	4 6 ☑ +	15 ☒	24 ☐	33 ☐ = ☐	16
Accountability	3 7 ☑ +	16 ☐	25 ☐	34 ☐ = ☐	14
Cross Cultural Sensitivity	4 8 ☐ +	17 ☐	26 ☐	35 ☐ = ☐	17
Managing Conflict	3 9 ☐ +	18 ☐	27 ☐	36 ☐ = ☐	13

Add the skill effectiveness scores for each dimension to get your Overall Effectiveness score. **145**

(continued on next page)

WORKSHEET 6.1
Your Skill Scores

What Your Scores Mean

The Team Leader Self Assessment is designed to assess your use of the skills and behaviors that are essential to effectively leading a team.

Your overall effectiveness score will give you a general picture of how well you use these skills and behaviors. This score will range between 180 (most effective) and 36 (least effective).

Your skill effectiveness scores will indicate how well you perform the nine dimensions associated with effectively leading a team. Each of these scores will range between 20 (most effective) and 4 (least effective).

The Effectiveness Score ranges chart below will help you interpret more accurately your overall and skill effectiveness scores. The chart categorizes all effectiveness scores into the ranges of "Strength," "Competent" and "Development Need." Locate your scores on the chart and circle the range of numbers within which each of your scores falls. The Overall Effectiveness column of the chart will help you better interpret your overall effectiveness scores. The Skill Effectiveness columns of the chart are designed to help you gain a more accurate picture of your strengths and development needs on each of the nine dimensions critical to leading effective teams.

Take a moment to notice whether your scores fall above or below competent. If you have scores that fall into the "Strength" category either overall or on any of the nine team leader dimensions, congratulations! These scores show that you use the skills and behaviors in these areas significantly more effectively than average.

On the other hand, if you have scores in either the "Competent" or "Development Need" categories, these identify areas where there is room for improvement, with scores in the "Development Need" category having the highest priority.

Effectiveness Score Ranges

	Open and Clear Communication	Problem Solving and Decision Making	Cooperative Relationships	Goal Oriented	Trust	Relationship with Management	Accountability	Cross Cultural Sensitivity	Managing Conflict	Overall Effectiveness
Strength	16-20	16-20	16-20	16-20	16-20	16-20	16-20	16-20	16-20	144-180
Competent	11-15	11-15	11-15	11-15	11-15	11-15	11-15	11-15	11-15	91-143
Development Need	4-10	4-10	4-10	4-10	4-10	4-10	4-10	4-10	4-10	36-90

WORKSHEET 6.2
Team Member Self-Assessment

Note

Please keep in mind that the results from this inventory will be helpful to you only to the extent that they are an accurate reflection of your actual team member behavior. Therefore, it is to your benefit to respond as candidly as possible.

Instructions

- The inventory consists of 36 statements that describe a team member's behavior with his or her team.

- Carefully read the first statement. Keeping in mind your own team member behavior, indicate how often you engage in the behavior along a continuum from *Never* to *Always*.

- Place an X in the circle that corresponds to your choice for each statement. Place an X in only one circle per statement. You must make a choice for all 36 statements in order for the assessment to be scored accurately.

- Make your choices based on how you actually behave, not on how you think you should behave.

		NEVER				ALWAYS
1.	During team discussions, I like to have both myself and the other team members take charge.	①	②	③	④	⑤
2.	When solving problems, I avoid "knee-jerk" reactions and help the team find the root cause of the problem before taking action.	①	②	③	④	⑤
3.	I help create an atmosphere where all team members respect one another and enjoy working together.	①	②	③	④	⑤
4.	I help my fellow team members understand the reasons for having the goals we do.	①	②	③	④	⑤
5.	I make an effort to get to know all my fellow team members as individuals.	①	②	③	④	⑤
6.	I make a point to keep my team leader informed about what is happening with the team and any successes we've had.	①	②	③	④	⑤
7.	When working on team tasks, I strive to keep my commitments and consistently do what I've agreed to.	①	②	③	④	⑤
8.	I respect and effectively use the differences in style, culture, and competence of all the members of our team.	①	②	③	④	⑤
9.	When differences arise during team meetings, I try to get the opposing team members to understand and state the points of view of the other.	①	②	③	④	⑤
10.	I strive to create an atmosphere of open, two-way communication between myself and my fellow team members.	①	②	③	④	⑤

(continued on next page)

STEP **6**

		NEVER				ALWAYS
11.	When a problem is identified, I share equally with my fellow team members in solving it.	①	②	③	④	⑤
12.	I help create an atmosphere where all team members recognize and praise one another for their specific accomplishments.	①	②	③	④	⑤
13.	I help in the setting of team goals and milestones in order to create a feeling of commitment and ownership.	①	②	③	④	⑤
14.	I strive to develop a positive and supportive relationship with all my fellow team members.	①	②	③	④	⑤
15.	When team accomplishments are recognized, I make sure the entire team is recognized and not just selected individuals.	①	②	③	④	⑤
16.	I provide regular feedback to my fellow team members to reinforce things they've done well and point out things that need improvement.	①	②	③	④	⑤
17.	During team discussions, I help ensure that every team member has an opportunity to state his or her point of view and have it listened to and considered, even if it differs from the norm.	①	②	③	④	⑤
18.	When differences arise during team meetings, I try to keep communication open, candid, and unguarded between the opposing team members.	①	②	③	④	⑤
19.	During team discussions, I respect the ideas offered by my fellow team members and listen to them without interruption.	①	②	③	④	⑤

STEP **6**

		NEVER				ALWAYS
20.	When solving team problems, I use a systematic, no-blame approach to problem solving and decision-making.	①	②	③	④	⑤
21.	I help create an atmosphere where all team members recognize that they need one another's knowledge, skills, and abilities to successfully complete team tasks.	①	②	③	④	⑤
22.	I formally and informally demonstrate a strong professional commitment to achieving our team goals.	①	②	③	④	⑤
23.	I make it known that I'm available to help if any of my fellow team members encounter difficulties accomplishing a task.	①	②	③	④	⑤
24.	I keep my team leader informed on the status of team projects and what additional resources (time, money, equipment, support), if any, are needed to complete the projects.	①	②	③	④	⑤
25.	I provide regular feedback to my fellow team members to help them understand what standards of behavior and performance are and are not acceptable.	①	②	③	④	⑤
26.	During team discussions, I refuse to participate in any conversations that may be perceived by my fellow team members as derogatory or offensive.	①	②	③	④	⑤
27.	When differences arise during team discussions, I help the opposing team members discover and state explicitly the common interest and goals that they share.	①	②	③	④	⑤

(continued on next page)

STEP
6

	SKILL ASSESSMENT				
	NEVER				ALWAYS

28.	During team discussions, I acknowledge each team member's point of view and ask questions to get more information.	①	②	③	④	⑤
29.	When solving team problems, I use an approach marked by timely decision-making without procrastination and an appropriate bias toward action.	①	②	③	④	⑤
30.	I help create an atmosphere where all team members are helpful and supportive of one another.	①	②	③	④	⑤
31.	I encourage my fellow team members to feel proud each time we achieve one of our goals.	①	②	③	④	⑤
32.	I keep my promises and respond promptly and willingly to requests from my fellow team members.	①	②	③	④	⑤
33.	I am sensitive to the many pressures faced by upper management and use this perspective to help my fellow team members understand why management makes some of the decisions they do.	①	②	③	④	⑤
34.	When working on team tasks, I willingly face up to my mistakes and accept responsibility for what happened.	①	②	③	④	⑤
35.	If another team member makes a remark or joke that could be perceived as derogatory or offensive, I intervene and point out that such behavior is not appropriate.	①	②	③	④	⑤
36.	During discussions of differences, I help the opposing team members focus on joint problem solving and identify solutions that are satisfactory to both parties.	①	②	③	④	⑤

WORKSHEET 6.2
Your Skill Scores

Instructions

- Listed below are the nine dimensions associated with effective team leadership. Numbers to the right represent statements from the assessment. Refer back to statement number one and in the box labeled "1" below, enter the numerical value of the response you chose for that statement. For example, let's say that for statement one you marked a "3." In this case, you would enter a 3 in the box labeled "1" below.
- Total the numerical values on each dimension to obtain your skill effectiveness scores.
- After finding your skill effectiveness scores on each dimension, total your scores to determine your Overall Effectiveness.

Dimensions	Statements	Skill Effectiveness
Opening and Clear Communication	1 [3] + 10 [4] + 19 [3] + 28 [5]	= 15
Problem Solving and Decision-Making	2 [3] + 11 [4] + 20 [3] + 29 [3]	= 13
Cooperative Relationships	3 [4] + 12 [4] + 21 [3] + 30 [4]	= 15
Goal Oriented	4 [3] + 13 [4] + 22 [4] + 31 [4]	= 15
Trust	5 [5] + 14 [4] + 23 [3] + 32 [4]	= 16
Relationship With Management	6 [5] + 15 [3] + 24 [4] + 33 [3]	= 15
Accountability	7 [5] + 16 [4] + 25 [3] + 34 [4]	= 16
Cross Cultural Sensitivity	8 [4] + 17 [5] + 26 [5] + 35 [5]	= 19
Managing Conflict	9 [3] + 18 [4] + 27 [3] + 36 [3]	= 13

Add the skill effectiveness scores for each dimension to get your Overall Effectiveness score.   137

(continued on next page)

STEP 6

WORKSHEET 6.2

Your Skill Scores

What Your Scores Mean

The Team Member Self-Assessment is designed to assess your use of the skills and behaviors that are essential to effectively working on a team.

Your overall effectiveness score will give you a general picture of how well you use these skills and behaviors. This score will range between 180 (most effective) and 36 (least effective).

Your skill effectiveness scores will indicate how well you perform each of the nine dimensions associated with effectively working on a team. Each of these scores will range between 20 (most effective) and 4 (least effective).

The Effectiveness Score ranges chart below will help you interpret more accurately your overall and skill effectiveness scores. The chart categorizes all effectiveness scores into the ranges of "Strength," "Competent" and "Development Need." Locate your scores on the chart and circle the range of numbers within which each of your scores falls. The Overall Effectiveness column of the chart will help you better interpret your overall effectiveness score. The Skill Effectiveness columns of the chart are designed to help you gain a more accurate picture of your strengths and development needs on each of the nine dimensions critical to effectively working on a team.

Take a moment to notice whether your scores fall above or below "Competent." If you have scores that fall into the "Strength" category either overall or on any of the nine dimensions, congratulations! These scores show that you use the skills and behaviors in these areas significantly more effectively than average.

On the other hand, if you have scores in either the "Competent" or "Development Need" categories, these identify areas where there is room for improvement, with scores in the "Development Need" category having the highest priority.

Effectiveness Score Ranges

	Open and Clear Communication	Problem Solving and Decision Making	Cooperative Relationships	Goal Oriented	Trust	Relationship with Management	Accountability	Cross Cultural Sensitivity	Managing Conflict	Overall Effectiveness
Strength	16-20	16-20	16-20	16-20	16-20	16-20	16-20	16-20	16-20	144-180
Competent	11-15	11-15	11-15	11-15	11-15	11-15	11-15	11-15	11-15	91-143
Development Need	4-10	4-10	4-10	4-10	4-10	4-10	4-10	4-10	4-10	36-90

WORKSHEET 6.3
ANALYZING YOUR SCORES

Instructions

- Refer back either to your Team Leader Self-Assessment or Team Member Self-Assessment Effectiveness Score Ranges chart.

- Note your highest and lowest scores.

- Think about your role either as a team leader or team member and answer the following questions.

Action Planning

1. What are your overall reactions to your scores?

2. Which results please you most?

3. How would you like to see your scores improved?

4. What steps can you take to improve your scores?

5. What obstacles might keep you from taking the steps listed above and how can you overcome them?

Tap Into Creative Energy of the Team to Develop Innovative Approaches

OVERVIEW

Get out of left-brain thinking

Create a new environment

Turn creativity into innovation

Use creativity and innovation daily

If you always think what you always thought, you will always get what you always got.

—Gerald Haman

STEP **7**

Innovation is vital to the health of organizations and to the functioning of successful work teams. As noted earlier in this book, teams naturally stick to familiar practices they know to be successful. And, of course, that makes perfect sense. But imagine what might happen if a team sought better ways of working and constantly searched for new efficiencies. Certainly, greater results would follow. So what does innovation mean in a team environment? How do you get your team to access its creative energies and take advantage of the benefits of innovation? Consider this situation.

The annual sales meeting planning committee had been meeting weekly every Monday morning for a month or more. Everyone takes a turn and gives updates, just like always. I don't particularly want to be here—I have done my tasks and am annoyed that some others haven't met their deadlines—again. And they are asking for help from the team to complete what they should have done already. Next, the leader asks for ideas for an ice breaker activity to conduct during the first evening reception. He's looking for something to get people interacting across functions—something to prevent marketing people talking only to marketing people, sales people only to sales people, customer service people only to customer service people, and so on. No one can think of anything. There is no energy in the room. Our only ideas are what we have done before.

What do we need here? We need energy, ideas, and some good questions! Initial ideas stimulate more ideas because ideas generate other thoughts, which in turn generate more ideas! That is the way it works. Have you tried to think of a solution and come up with nothing, but as soon as you talk to someone else the ideas start popping? This is one of the advantages of a team—having other people to bounce ideas off of.

Let's start by looking at the difference between creativity and innovation. Creativity is all about generating new ideas—it means thinking outside the box. Innovation is the act of using these new ideas to create something that did not exist before. Innovation puts creativity into action.

Many techniques exist to increase creativity on your team. This step in building effective teams describes some paths to take to foster team creativity and innovation.

Get Out of Left-Brain Thinking

Our left brain is very important. Most of us spend large amounts of time using the left side of our brain. It deals with structure, logic, analysis, and getting things done in a linear fashion. Although it is efficient, left-brain thinking can be a roadblock to creative thinking. So how do you and your team engage your creative right brain? Here are some ideas to spur creative thinking on your team.

Capture Your Ideas

Carry a notebook to capture ideas to bring to team meetings and brainstorming sessions. Thomas Edison carried an idea book with him all the time. The book was not simply his "to do" list. He carried the book to capture ideas when they occurred to him during his day whether walking down the street or taking a break sitting on a park bench. Remember, creative thinking requires relaxed time and space for the ideas to surface. Make sure everyone on the team understands that creativity does not happen when you are heads-down working and stressed out trying to meet a deadline (Caldecott 2008).

Capturing ideas can be accomplished in a variety of other ways as well. Bulleted lists on a flipchart are useful and efficient. But why not try capturing ideas in a nonlinear way, perhaps in a random pattern or a circle?

For example, Figure 7.1 shows how a team might plan a social function such as a holiday party. First, the group looked at the major tasks to be completed then added details as they thought of them. Visual images help stimulate additional ideas and illustrate potential relationships.

Figure 7.2 depicts a brainstorming activity. As the team generates ideas, the facilitator writes down the ideas in random patterns and makes connections when possible. Using this graphic method to capture ideas gets thinking out of the left brain and accesses the creativity of the right brain. In this figure the examples of random notes generated in a brainstorming session are organized after a team discussion.

Using a graphic method to capture ideas and organize them is known as mindmapping. If you Google the phrase you will find hundreds of articles and resources that will help you use this method

STEP **7**

FIGURE 7.1

Example of a Nonlinear Idea Capture

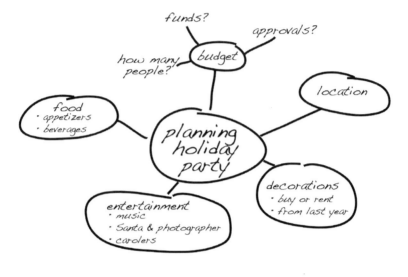

effectively. Visually portraying ideas clearly helps with problem solving, jump-starts initial brainstorming sessions, and drives solution thinking. Remember the old adage, "A picture is worth a thousand words." Visuals help you get from creative ideas to innovations you can implement.

Root-Cause Mapping

If your team is trying to find the root cause of a problem or trying to fix a broken process, you should consider using a tree visual as a way to kick-start team discussion. As you can see, the visual is a great way of showing relationships and how processes and people can help you know what action to take first. You do not need to be an artist to use this technique. You just need to get the point across. Besides, as another old adage goes, "If it is in the fruit, it is in the root." See Figure 7.3 for an example of a root diagram.

FIGURE 7.2

An Example of a Mindmap

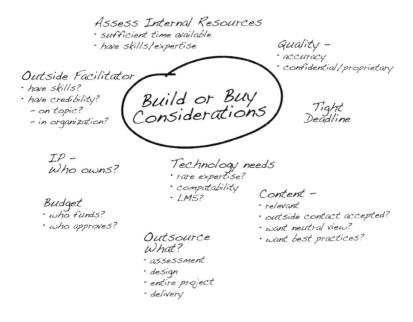

Create a New Environment

Another way to stimulate your team's collective right brain is to change the look of "meetings." It is easy for the same people to meet in the same room and do the same things—you get stuck in a rut. A rut is a coffin with the ends cut out. Break the routine! Innovation and creativity are hard pressed to thrive in a rut.

Make the meeting environment stimulating. Occasionally change the meeting room and other things about the meeting. This can mean you try a different food, have a theme, dress differently. Decorate the meeting room with a theme for the purpose of stimulating ideas on a topic. If you are planning a global meeting, plan to serve food from the different countries attending. These differences can be subtle or dramatic. It is all about expressing creativity.

STEP 7

FIGURE 7.3

An Example of a Root Diagram

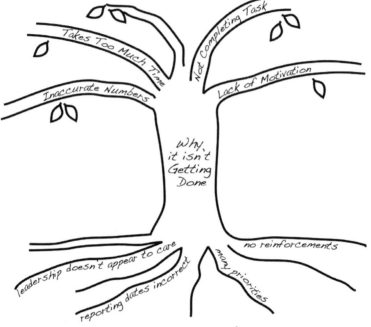

Takes Too Much Time

Not Completing Task

Inaccurate Numbers

Lack of Motivation

Why, it isn't Getting Done

leadership doesn't appear to care

reporting dates incorrect

many priorities

no reinforcements

If it is in the fruit, it's in the root!

Here are some questions that can generate thoughts for creating an idea-generating environment.

◆ How would you describe an environment that stimulates ideas?

◆ What small changes can you make to the current environment to make it more appealing?

◆ What changes would stimulate people visually?

◆ How can you use sound or music to soothe or stimulate?

◆ How can you use taste or fragrance to help create the environment you are looking for?

◆ What environments are comfortable to you?

POINTER

For Team Members

People have natural ups and downs when it comes to creativity. Some are more in touch than others.

Support your teammates when they need it. Ask them questions like:

◆ What do you want?

◆ What do you wish for?

◆ What do you need?

◆ How would your team describe the desired environment?

◆ Would you want colors that are stimulating or soothing?

Not all ideas will be practical or affordable, but it is good to think of ways to stimulate people—even if only occasionally. You can even break a virtual team out of a rut—try brainstorming via webcast or in a socialnetworking site like Second Life.

POINTER

Four Stages to Innovation

◆ Investigate needs

◆ Create ideas

◆ Evaluate solutions

◆ Activate plans

STEP 7

Turn Creativity Into Innovation

Now that we've covered some ways to engage the creative right brain, how do we turn that creativity into innovation—something new and different that we can work with? Gerald Haman, a leader in innovative thinking, recommends a four-stage approach to innovation (2009):

Stage 1: Investigate Needs

This approach fully describes the problem or challenge ahead of you. Thoroughly completing the research in this stage is important to the rest of the process. Short cuts taken here can impede progress later on. Here are some questions to help determine your needs:

- What is the problem or challenge you face?
- Who is your audience?
- What do you know and what do you need to find out?
- What is our plan to learn what we don't know?
- Who needs to know?
- Who will resist?

Stage 2: Create Ideas

Based on your problem, challenge, or mission, stage 2 is the period of idea generation. This is when ideas are generated as possible solutions. There are many ways to create new ideas. Brainstorming is one of the most common team approaches used to create ideas.

A typical brainstorming session takes place when the team comes together in one place (generally in person) to begin working on solutions to a problem. A leader presents and frames the situation or problem, and then lays the ground rules for all who are participating. The rules are normally simple: Any and all ideas are welcome and will be written down without judgment or editing. The goal is to generate ideas first and evaluate second. The benefit of doing an activity like this as a group—as a team—is that the ideas may begin slowly but will multiply as things get going.

Most of us have been involved in some type of brainstorming activity, whether in a formal business setting to decide on a new sales strategy or through involvement in some type of community-improvement program. Generally the group leader solicits ideas from those in attendance, and these ideas are captured on a white board or a flipchart. The ideas are then categorized and discussed, and the best approach to take is determined. Thomas Edison offers two excellent ideas to jump-start a brainstorming session, which can be run by anyone on your team whether or not she or he is an experienced facilitator:

◆ **Analogical Thinking**—Compare two different unrelated items, like your job and a light bulb, Lake Michigan and Shakespeare, innovation and potato chips, radio waves and pasta. Discussing the two items yields a list of everything these seemingly unrelated items have in common. The exercise is fun and spurs thinking outside the box.

Here is an example. Think about two different and unrelated items, like flip-flops and computers. Both are man-made, useful, and part of daily life. Each can be used by kids or adults, they come in different colors and styles, and are made by different manufacturers. You can buy cheap brands or higher quality versions, both are available worldwide. See what we mean?

◆ **Alternative Uses**—Ask participants to think of an item like a paper clip or a brick. The exercise asks those partici-pating to think of all the uses for these items that they can in one minute. The uses do not have to be practical. The point is to make a quick list of everything that comes to mind. Teams or team partners create these lists as an ex-ercise to effectively warm up the brain before the brain-storming session begins (Caldecott 2008).

STEP 7

No matter how you decide to begin your team brainstorming session or capture ideas, it is important not to judge or evaluate any idea offered by the team. Just listen and list the items as they are mentioned by the participants. Thomas Edison preferred to gen-erate ideas first, and organize them later. Your preferred method of generating or capturing ideas is not important. The greatest value of the brainstorming exercise lies in the number of ideas your team can generate and how the activity will inspire creativity. You might find that some teams are able to discuss a couple of options, pick one and then move on. Often, this is an appropriate path, and the best option is chosen despite the short amount of time spent brainstorming. If you have a limited amount of time, team facilitators can ask individual team members to bring ideas to the meeting.

Here are additional tips for a successful team brainstorming session:

◆ **Make sure the group is not judging ideas.** Engender a "blue sky" environment that accepts all ideas. The wilder the better. You never know when a seemingly wacky idea will lead to new and better solution.

◆ **Provide tactile items to keep team members' hands busy during brainstorming.** Busy hands help engage the brain and encourage creativity. Examples of creativity triggers include pipe cleaners, stress balls, Koosh balls, crayons and paper, and Silly Putty. Many other choices are called fiddlers (keeping active hands busy) and are available at www.trainerswarehouse.com.

◆ **Start with an ice breaker or energizer to help start the creative process.**

◆ **Use questions to help motivate the process.**
  ◆ What might be changed or improved?
  ◆ What might be combined, adapted, or recycled?
  ◆ How might other people approach this problem?
  ◆ What is at risk?
  ◆ What are the possibilities?

Stage 3: Evaluate Solutions

During this stage we will take all those wonderful ideas and filter them. What are the possible solutions? Which ones will best solve the problem or challenge? Questions that will help with this stage:

◆ What are the evaluation criteria?
◆ What are the potential investments for each solution?
◆ When considering the investment and return-on-investment, which are the best solutions?
◆ Why or how could solutions fail?
◆ Who needs to be sold on the solutions?

With these questions answered, you can filter your solutions down to the best possible solution.

Stage 4: Activate Plans

This is the fun part (at least for me!). This is where you take the best solution and figure out how you are going to make it happen! Here are some helpful questions to begin this stage:

◆ What are the next steps and what are our plans for it?
◆ Who should do what by when?
◆ What obstacles do we expect and how will we overcome them?
◆ How will we track or monitor progress?
◆ Who should champion these plans?

Once you have completed stage 4, you will have the plans in place to accomplish your goal!

Use Creativity and Innovation Daily

Now that we have discussed some ideas to try to generate creativity, the big question is: How do we make creativity part of team behavior and not something to turn to occasionally when you have a problem to solve? Here's a quick list of some ideas that will keep creativity alive and kicking on your team:

◆ **Use it or lose it.** Regularly include an "out there" idea-generation exercise in every meeting to keep your team's right brain in shape.
◆ **Make visuals part of every meeting.** Have a flipchart or a whiteboard. Use a projector while capturing ideas on a computer. Use color and make all ideas available for everyone to see. Ideas stimulate ideas.
◆ **Inspire up**. Ask your team what would inspire them now. Thinking off topic may clear the thought processes and make way for creativity and innovation.
◆ **Get unstuck.** Be prepared to use creative approaches if your team's problem-solving ability gets stuck (use mind-mapping techniques).

Keep in mind that encouraging creativity outside of work can help keep it mainstream while at work. Here are some ideas to continually generate variety that often inspire creativity:

- Add some spice to your living space or wardrobe. It doesn't have to be expensive.
- Deliberately connect with your inner child. Color with kids. Swing at the park. Drink grape Kool-Aid. Eat Jello Jigglers.
- Connect with the arts. Read poetry. See an artsy movie. Go to an art museum. Connect with art or music in a different way than you normally would.
- Break your routine! Take a different route to work. Go to a new store. Remember, a rut is a coffin with the ends cut out.
- Try a different food or snack. Go to an Indian restaurant or try some other ethnic cuisine.
- Doodle in color.
- Write with a different color of ink.
- Start with a daily devotional or meditation.

POINTER

For Team Leaders

The number-one thing a leader can do to stimulate creativity and innovation on a team is to model it. If you ever say to yourself, "I'm not creative," stop it. Change it to, "I'm working on my creativity to stimulate innovation." If your team sees that you value creativity and innovation, and are trying new things yourself, this will encourage them to be creative as well.

Keep the Questions Coming

Asking good questions also keeps creativity flowing. Try both random and planned questions:

- What needs to happen for us to move forward?
- What do we need to know, feel, see, and do?

Energizer and Ice Breaker Example

Include a fictional-products activity in your process. In this activity the team takes on the name of a fictional product such as Orange Blast, Bling Bling, Square Zero, Cup of Life. Ask the group questions such as:

◆ What is the product?
◆ What is its slogan or ad?
◆ Who would be the celebrity spokesperson for it?

Teams or small groups really like this exercise. It stimulates creativity while simultaneously increasing group energy and participation.

◆ What does "good" look like?
◆ What resources are available that might be helpful?
◆ What do we fear?
◆ What surprises can we prepare for?
◆ How do we see this as an opportunity rather than a problem?

Make It Happen!

Believe it or not, we are all innately creative. Some of us just need a bit of help to access these creative tendencies. Some team members will feel self-conscious about being more creative. As a team, decide on the benefits of creativity and, as a group, answer these key questions. The answers may surprise you.

◆ What can the leader do to stimulate creativity?
◆ Is there a creative way the team can work together?
◆ Can communication be creative?
◆ Is there an innovative way to build relationships?
◆ Can the group work innovatively to be more efficient?
◆ Is there a creative solution to a problem?
◆ How can the group creatively celebrate success?

Organizational culture *is* an important factor to consider when developing ideas to add creativity and innovation approaches to your team. A very conservative culture may not be comfortable with hoola hoops and crayons, but using techniques such as mindmaps or creative meeting strategies might be acceptable. Whatever the culture, it is important to stretch the boundaries, if possible. Make time to introduce stimulating activities to your team and adopt some "rut busting" behaviors. Support team members on their journey to be more creative and lead the team in innovative exercising.

Use Virtual Team Techniques Effectively

Virtual teams aren't about technology, they are about the people. Technology is supporting the person-to-person communication and person-to-person interactions.

—Trish Uhl

It's 5 a.m. and dark outside. Inside, the glow of the computer monitor and the backlight on the cell phone provide the illumination. There are some voices talking somewhere, but there aren't any faces connected with them. Suddenly there's a pause and you realize that the voices were talking to you and are now waiting for your response. Is this a dream? Are you part of an alien adventure movie? No, this is your weekly team-status meeting. Welcome to the realities of working on a virtual team.

Starting a new project has always created questions: How will I introduce myself? What will my role be? Which approach will we take in tackling this project? What are the other team members like? Working with team members in different geographic locations creates other questions: What time zones and "business" hours do they keep? How will we communicate and function as a team—a virtual team?

Whether you are a team leader who is managing people remotely, or you are a participating team member, working virtually can be challenging. Fortunately, there are established tools and techniques to keep your virtual team on track.

Define a Framework for Virtual Teaming

Let's start with the basics—What is a virtual team? According to Jessica Lipnack and Jeffrey Stamps, authors of books about people networks and virtual teaming, a virtual team is "a group of people who work interdependently with a shared purpose across space, time, and organization boundaries using technology" (Lipnack & Stamps 2000).

There are many different configurations of virtual teams. Identifying the type of virtual team you're on can help you understand team dynamics and address the unique challenges of each type of team. The seven types of virtual teams described here are adapted from *Mastering Virtual Teams: Strategies, Tools, and Techniques That Succeed* (Duarte & Snyder 1999):

- ◆ **Networked teams** consist of individuals who collaborate frequently across time, distance, and organizational structures to achieve a common goal or purpose. Team members rotate on and off the team as their expertise is needed, which means it's often unclear as to who is on the team and who is not at any given point in time.
- ◆ **Parallel teams** carry out special assignments, tasks, or functions that the regular organization does not want or is not equipped to perform. Parallel teams are also used when expertise does not reside in one location or one organization. Parallel teams differ from networked teams in that parallel team members are clearly identified.

What Is Co-Location?

Wikipedia's definition of *co-location* (also collocation) is "the act of placing multiple (sometimes related) entities within a single location." This term refers to people who work together at the same facility as well as those who physically work together within close proximity to each other, such as in the same room. The purpose of co-location is to facilitate communication and teamwork by offering easy opportunities for information sharing, collaborative problem solving, and relationship building.

◆ **Project or product development teams** also cross time, distance, and organizational boundaries. These teams complete projects for users or customers for a defined, but extended, period of time.

◆ **Work, functional, or production teams** perform regular and ongoing assignments.

◆ **Service teams** support customers or the internal organization typically in an around-the-clock service or technical-support role.

◆ **Management teams** work collaboratively on a daily basis within a functional division of a corporation to lead corporate activities.

◆ **Action teams** deal with immediate action, often in emergency situations. They differ from all of the other types of teams in that they are usually formed only to meet a specific and urgent need.

What these teams have in common with co-located teams is that team members must communicate and collaborate to get work done. The challenges and solutions are similar; you need to adjust accordingly.

STEP **8**

Determine Elements of Successful Virtual Teaming

Success can be defined as the team's ability to produce interdependent work that meets the defined success criteria of the project. Taking it a step further, success not only means meeting the project success criteria, but also giving the team members a feeling of satisfaction and completion—a feeling that their time and effort are well spent. So success is achieved when the team works together to produce the desired results and feels good about the outcome—just as with more traditional teams.

In truth, virtual teamwork is 90 percent about the people and only 10 percent about the technology. We've discussed all of the foundational elements in previous parts of this book—selecting team leads, clarifying tasks and roles, setting the foundation for solid communication, building trust, establishing and maintaining healthy relationships. Reliance on trust, communication, and building/supporting interpersonal relationships are necessary to all teams (Kostner 1996).

The trick here is to learn how to successfully build these foundational elements in virtual environments. We often think of the logistic challenges (varying languages, time zones, and cultures) but not about how virtual environments can negatively affect team success. Challenges for virtual teams are similar to those other teams face and can include

◆ **Unfamiliar power structure**—Many people in organizations still identify with "command and control" power structures in which one person is designated as the leader. Virtual teams often require shared leadership, in which all team members share in the ownership and responsibility of making decisions and seeing the work through to completion. The team lead role is less about authority, and more about fostering trust, working toward clear communication, and driving toward a shared vision.

- ◆ **No shared history**—Virtual teams often start out as a group of strangers without the traditional social cues that come with co-location. People are not sure who to trust, how to collaborate, or how to communicate. This presents the absence of a familiar framework from which to solve problems and make decisions.

- ◆ **Lack of familiarity**—The uncertainty that comes with new situations can lead to increased sensitivity to communication as well as interpersonal and cultural factors. Until team members become acquainted with each other, misunderstanding the other party's intent can amplify problems and conflicts.

- ◆ **Varying contexts**—People working in separate locations not only have access to different information but also send and receive information in different contexts, oftentimes resulting in mixed signals and miscommunication.

- ◆ **Lack of human contact**—Isolation can decrease team spirit, trust, and productivity.

- ◆ **Competing local and/or project demands**—The virtual team is not the organizational "home" for the participants; rather, it is a structure they use to accomplish their jobs or the demands of a project. When the pressure is on, virtual teamwork is often overshadowed by local demands or can be overridden by the demands of another project.

Addressing these challenges requires commitment to the team and its purpose. This, in turn, requires some level of trust, which is based on team members' openness and knowledge of each other. An article in the *Harvard Management Update*, "The Art of Managing Virtual Teams: Eight Key Lessons," again underscores the importance of trust.

According to the article, team members who exchanged "get acquainted" messages at the beginning of the project tended to communicate better and more often throughout the life of the project. These communications included regular discussions of individual

STEP **8**

goals and schedules. Virtual team members then worked to help each other meet the goals. Team members who had initiated and responded to interpersonal communications at the outset of the project were quicker to confront nonperformers and more likely to get their work done on time.

Team leads and managers were not excluded from these interactions. They worked hard to clarify objectives and ensure team members understood their roles on the team. These interactions "led to a stable project environment where people could build working relationships" (Wardell 1998). The better the relationships, the more work is accomplished.

Virtual team leaders and members can learn from these lessons:

◆ **Walk before you run.** Managers who can't successfully manage conventional teams probably can't manage virtual teams.

◆ **Light a fire in the belly**. A virtual team needs a clear mission.

◆ **Assume nothing**. Spell out everything.

◆ **Megacommunicate**. Once a project starts, the manager has to help people keep from feeling isolated. You need to touch the team every day—by email or phone, or a posting to a website, and so on. The leader must encourage team members to keep in touch with each other. Familiarity breeds trust, and people who trust one another will inevitably produce more.

◆ **Find allies**. You are often competing for team members' time because they are frequently assigned to multiple projects, so you have to establish working relationships with their managers.

◆ **Compensate creatively**. Base incentives on project and personal performance. Ask each team member what he/she wants out of the project.

◆ **Watch for conflict—and learn how to manage it.** Phone conversations are a good time to probe for problems.

◆ **Do better next time**. Conduct a detailed postmortem.

Notice how these lessons have little to do with technology and have everything to do with people, communication, and trust. Technology can, however, be used to foster trust and enable communication.

Implement Virtual Team Tools

Creating solutions for virtual teams can be a strategic advantage to your organization. Complexity is involved in building successful virtual teams because effective solutions need to blend people, process, and technology. Implementing effective virtual teams also means more upfront preparation, careful thought, and ongoing energy to be successful.

In virtual environments, trust, communication, and community don't just happen because you deploy a new technology. Software applications can help to facilitate conversation and working relationships, but they are only tools—you must still be part of the conversation and cultivate the community. Virtual relationships require time and energy just as the co-located relationships do. Virtual teaming adds a layer of difficulty because we have to think about it more—and be more deliberate in our interactions. Fortunately, technology provides cost-effective solutions for creating environments where we can meet, collaborate, exercise our interpersonal skills, trust, and be trusted. (For tips and activities for use with virtual teams, see Appendix D. A virtual teams glossary is there as well.)

Email

Although email has its place, it can be one of the worst tools when used for communication, collaboration, and knowledge management. Email is designed to handle one-sided conversations for a limited audience. This is appropriate for private messages but doesn't always work well for general team communication.

Social software is designed for open communication and team collaboration so everyone on the team has a voice. Consider the

Virtual Team Tools

- Meeting and Communication Tools
  - Webinar
  - Instant messaging
  - Video conferencing
  - Collaboration Tools
  - Wikis
  - Groupware / Team website
- Information-Sharing Tools
  - Discussion boards
  - Calendar
  - File Sharing
  - Information-Broadcasting Tools
  - Email
  - Blog
  - Podcast
  - RSS feeds
- Information-Gathering Tools
  - Surveys
  - Polls
  - Time Tracking
  - Social Networks
  - Facebook, Twitter, LinkedIn
- 3-D / Immersive Internet Environments
  - Second Life

See glossary in Appendix D for definitions of commonly used terms for virtual teams.

examples of supporting team activity via email versus a social software application shown in Table 8.1.

Email is also limited in its ability to foster relationships because it actually lets you "hide." For example, there is a tendency

TABLE 8.1
Email Effectiveness Versus Social Software

Team Tasks	Email Software	Social Software (Wiki)
Document collaboration	Exchanging a number of revised documents back and forth as email attachments often leads to full inboxes, confusion around document versions, and lost team member comments and changes. Frustrating!	Wikis allow multiple authors and editors to collaborate on one or more documents simultaneously. Wikis provide a centralized repository for all document revisions (making it easy to keep track of the latest changes) and help to keep large attachments out of your email inbox.
Scheduling meetings and adding participants	With email, process includes scheduling the meeting, inviting participants, and emailing meeting agenda and collateral documents to participants. Adding participants is difficult as well because you must send meeting notice and related documents to new attendees.	Using a Wiki to centralize the documentation also means no distribution is necessary. Just ensure new participants and team members have access to the Wiki, and they then have instant access to the project materials.
Onboarding new team members	With email, you must ensure that new team members have access to relevant project-related emails as they join the team.	Centralized documentation also means no distribution is necessary. Just ensure new participants and team members have access to the Wiki, and they then have instant access to the project materials and communications.

(continued on next page)

STEP 8

Team Tasks	Email Software	Social Software (Wiki)
Transparent workspace (see work getting done)	NA	The team leader (as well as other team members) can see the work being done, which helps facilitate trust, encourages performance, and drives project engagement.

POINTER

When to Use Synchronous Versus Asynchronous Communication

◆ Urgent messages require synchronous dissemination so everyone receives the same information at the same time.

◆ Nonurgent messages (e.g., status updates) can be distributed using asynchronous technologies like blogs, wikis, discussion boards, or intranet pages.

for people to be more blunt in email than they would be in face-to-face communications. This is especially true for team members who have never met in person and who have little or no working relationship—it's easy not to think of the actual person on the receiving end of the message. Because of the poor communication medium and the lack of trust, issues can be amplified and escalate quickly.

Social Media Software

In addition to fostering open team communication and supporting interpersonal relationships, you can also use tools to build relationships and interaction. For example, sharing background, photos, and interests makes team members more human and less easily dismissed. Sharing member information also helps develop rapport among and between team members. It also provides a frame of reference and common ground for communicating in email, in person, and by phone.

Consider these tools and ideas for how to use them on your teams (see Table 8.2). Many of these tools have corporate counterparts that offer similar, if not identical, features. These enterprise versions can be installed behind the corporate firewall and managed internally (Suarez 2008).

Meeting Face-to-Face

As much as technology can help support the team effort, as the saying goes, sometimes "nothing beats being there." Co-location and face-to-face meetings are critical when

- ◆ holding the initial meeting to kickoff the team and launch the project
- ◆ discussing complex and/or major issues
- ◆ presenting results to internal and external clients.

An in-person meeting allows team members to get comfortable with each other's communication style while focusing on the work at hand. Not only does this allow people to interact within the context of the team and the task, it allows them to interact at breaks and sit together at meals and get to know each other. This is critical to establishing trusting and professional business relationships.

If you can't meet in person, try scheduling a video conference. From a psychological and sociological perspective, it is important for people to be able to visualize their teammates so they can become familiar with the person on the other side of the equipment.

If you cannot bring the team together face-to-face, or by video conference, do the best you can with the technology you have available to create a virtual meeting space that engages people on

STEP **8**

TABLE 8.2
Social Media Software Tools

Social Media Software	What Is It?	What Can I Do with It?
LinkedIn (Linkedin. com)	The purpose of the LinkedIn is to allow registered users to maintain a list of contact details of people they know and trust in business. The people in the list are called connections. Users can invite anyone (whether a site user or not) to become a connection. This list of connections can then be used in a number of ways: ◆ A contact network is built up consisting of direct connections, the connections of each of their connections (termed second-degree connections) and also the connections of second-degree connections (termed third-degree connections). This allows you to gain an introduction to someone you wish to know through a mutual, trusted contact. ◆ The information can then be used to find jobs, people, and business opportunities recommended by someone in one's contact network. ◆ Employers can list jobs and search for potential candidates. ◆ Job seekers can review the profile of hiring managers and discover which of their existing contacts can introduce them.	◆ Use the system as an internal team or project board where people can learn about each other, ask each other questions, create a shared team identity, and come to connect. Here's how: ◆ Each team member can create a profile - including a photo and a bit about each person's background and interests. ◆ The team can create a project team group. Information posted to the group is stored in a searchable, centralized location. You can use LinkedIn Answers to search for solutions or ask team members questions to generate ideas. ◆ Team members can use the Status feature to let their peers know what they're working on and invite input. ◆ Team members can post links to work products they are proud of to showcase their skills and expertise (Kawasaki 2007).

Social Media Software	What Is It?	What Can I Do with It?
Facebook (Facebook. com)	Facebook is a social network site consisting of an electronic directory made up of individuals' names, photographs, preferences, and people connections. Facebook gives people the power to share and makes the world more open and connected. Millions of people use Facebook everyday to keep up with friends, upload an unlimited number of photos, share links and videos, and learn more about the people they meet.	◆ Team members can foster interpersonal relationships by using their Facebook profiles to connect with co-workers, customers, family, and friends. ◆ Facebook can provide a new home for conversations currently being conducted in email. This can decrease email inbox sizes, for example, by taking the exchange of personal photos out of email and placing them (appropriately) on Facebook. ◆ Team members can also post status here—so others know where that person is, or what someone is working on.
Twitter (Twitter. com)	Twitter is a free social-networking and micro-blogging service that allows its users to send and read other users' updates (otherwise known as tweets), which are text-based posts of up to 140 characters in length. Users can receive updates via the Twitter website, SMS (on their cell phones), RSS, or email, or through an application such as Tweetie and Facebook.	◆ Individual team members can subscribe to each other's "tweets" and receive messages as to what their colleagues are doing. ◆ The project itself could have a Twitter account. All team members could subscribe to it and receive ongoing project communications.

(continued on next page)

STEP **8**

Social Media Software	What Is It?	What Can I Do with It?
Second Life	Second Life is a 3-D virtual world created by its residents. A free client program called the Second Life Viewer enables its users, called residents, to interact with each other through avatars. residents can explore, meet other residents, socialize, participate in individual and group activities, and create and trade virtual property and services with one another, or travel throughout the world, which residents refer to as the grid.	◆ Second Life's 3-D, graphical interface makes it distinctly different from the other social software applications listed here, but its purpose is the same - to bring people together in a virtual environment for purposes of connection, communication, and collaboration. ◆ Second Life is most often used by project teams for practicing business activities, for learning events, and for hosting meetings. ◆ Second Life is often used in these capacities to visualize and share complex data and design prototype products.

multiple levels. For ideas on how to engage people in both in-person and virtual meetings, see Appendix D.

Leading a Virtual Team

Leading a virtual team has its own set of challenges. Luckily, others have blazed the trail before us. Here I've compiled some of the best tips I've found.

According to the book *Managing Virtual Teams*, the challenge for managers (and leaders) of multicultural teams is to build an atmosphere of camaraderie, mutual respect, effective communication, and productivity despite differing worldviews and physical environments (Duarte & Snyder 1999). In essence, as a team leader or manager, you must take a disparate group of people and cultures and develop a team that combines the best of each culture and the strengths that the individual team members bring with them.

Managers and team leaders can facilitate building a team culture by

- budgeting for periodic in-person meetings
- facilitating an open discussion about team expectations
- being explicit with rules and expectations
- encouraging social interaction
- being proactive
- recognizing both team and individual efforts
- providing a centralized repository for project information
- facilitating rapport building
- being considerate.

The *Harvard Management Update* outlines six steps to take to improve success in managing virtual teams (Ross 2006):

- **Create face time.**
- **Set clear goals and expectations.**
- **Make the work visible**. Another roadblock to trust occurs when team members don't know whether their distant colleagues are taking care of business.

STEP **8**

◆ **Provide ongoing feedback.** Managers who are perceived as fair and trustworthy are usually those who provide feedback on their performance to subordinates. As with your team down the hall, your virtual team needs regular input on how it is doing.

◆ **Showcase team members' competence.** When managing a virtual team, you must make sure each team member has a clear understanding of her/his role and, just as important, the roles of teammates. You must also make special efforts to highlight each individual's expertise for the rest of the team.

◆ **Foster cultural understanding.** When you are managing from afar, cultural differences stand out. Virtual teams must often overcome language barriers and diverse ways of doing business. When these kinds of differences aren't addressed and understood, it is very easy to dismiss or come to distrust a virtual colleague.

Send a consistent message about the value of teamwork. Here's a sample of some more guidelines (Ross 2006):

◆ **Strike the appropriate balance between yourself and your team.** Spell out the team's objectives but leave it up to the team members to decide how to achieve the goals.

◆ **Provide training in teamwork skills,** such as listening, communicating with different kinds of people, and staying focused on the task.

◆ **If at all possible, provide teams with opportunities to work together over a period of years.** After all, nothing teaches teamwork better than actual experience.

◆ **Encourage members to design metrics for assessing their performance.**

◆ **Set up a steering committee to monitor the work of teams in your organization.**

Make It Happen!

Devin Cobb says, "Virtual teams are there for each other." I couldn't have summed it up better myself!

When your team is having problems, the answer generally isn't to throw more technology at it. Team problems will generally be solved by the human factor. If you identify the human dynamics at play, you can evaluate or select the technology that can help you bridge that gap. For example, communication can be misunderstood or incomplete because people don't understand the intent of the message. When digging in deeper, you assess the situation and find people are missing the visual cues that go along with the message (because the communicating has been done via phone conference). Determine how you can provide the visual cues to team members and select the technology accordingly.

Being part of a virtual team presents many of the same challenges as more traditional teams—fostering an environment for open communication and trust, keeping the momentum going—as well as a few new ones. Fortunately there are myriad tools and tips available to help bridge the geographic divide. The tried-and-true rules for working on a team and building trust still apply, but

STEP 8

don't be afraid to try new ideas and new tools. Engage and share with your team members—it's more fun that way anyway. After all, positive things about working virtually include no one seeing the coffee stains on your shirt, not having to face that long and slow commute, not to mention occasionally being able to throw a load in the washer!

Deal with Team Problems and Move On

Top 10 problem areas and symptoms

Tips and techniques for working through problems

Group problem solving

Give me a lever long enough and I shall move the world.

—Archimedes

It is inevitable that teams will face conflicts, struggles, and obstacles. I have listed here the top 10 problems that teams encounter and the symptoms each presents. To increase your team's effectiveness, I recommend that you and your team members go through this list and identify any signs of potential problems that may exist on your team. Then refer to the corresponding discussion of each of these areas to check out tips and techniques to use to address these problems.

Top 10 Team Problems and Their Symptoms

1. **Lack of Clarity or Agreement on Team Mission**

    Symptoms:

    ◆ Team members cannot easily describe the team's mission.

    ◆ Contradictory team goals or action plans exist.

    ◆ Team lacks clear direction or focus.

STEP **9**

◆ Project goals are unrealistic (team mission is too broad or too narrow).

2. **Low Trust Levels Among Members**
Symptoms:
◆ Members withhold information from others.
◆ Members lack respect—there is a lot of talk but not much listening.
◆ Disagreements are aired in private discussions after meetings.
◆ Meeting atmosphere continues to be tense and uncomfortable.
◆ Hidden agendas are at work—certain members have ulterior motives that are not shared.

3. **Poor Team Communications Skills**
Symptoms:
◆ Some members dominate the discussions, while others say very little.
◆ Team has problems or issues that members refuse to talk about for fear of repercussions or a belief that nothing will change.
◆ There is confusion or disagreement about roles or work assignments.

4. **Poor Handling of Team Conflicts**
Symptoms:
◆ Team avoids dealing with personality conflicts or allows power struggles to continue.
◆ Cliques have formed—factions of team members exclude others on the team.
◆ Information is guarded or controlled by only a few team members.
◆ Team members work on action plans without the consent of the rest of the team.

5. **Poor Team Process**
Symptoms:
◆ Team is inflexible—some members discount or ignore contributions of other members to suit their own agendas.

- Team allows members with strong personalities to dominate the team process.
- Symptoms and not the root of the problem are addressed.
- Team members compromise to please the team.
- Decisions tend to be made by the team leader or one or two team members with little involvement from the other team members.

6. **Weak Senior Management/Sponsorship**
   Symptoms:
   - People outside the team are critical of the team and are not cooperating.
   - Outside managers pressure team members to "fudge the data."
   - Outside managers pressure team members to find "quick fixes."
   - Team members complain that they can't afford time on this team because of regular job priorities back in their departments.

7. **Lack of Accountability Among Team Members**
   Symptoms:
   - Poor follow-through—team members fail to complete assignments or meet deadlines.
   - There is a great deal of discussion but little progress toward accomplishing the goal.

8. **Team Is Overwhelmed by Work**
   Symptoms:
   - Team members complain that they have too much to do on the team.

9. **Wrong People on the Team**
   Symptoms:
   - The team is overloaded with people who all have the same team-player mentality or the same job expertise/ background.
   - People on the team have no content expertise or vested interest in the project.

10. **Team Is Too Quick to Find Solutions**
    Symptoms:
    ◆ Team members pressure the group to solve the problems
    quickly without adequate investment in analysis or
    researching the root of the problem or working through a
    variety of potential solutions.

Tips and Techniques for Working Through Common Team Problems

1. Lack of Clarity or Agreement on Team Mission

When it is difficult to understand what the team's main objective is
the team will flounder. Start with a clearly stated mission and begin the first team meetings using it. If needed, go back to the
stakeholder or steering committee and get clarification to create a
vision of what the expected outcome should be. A great exercise to
try is to go around the table and have each member describe her or
his understanding of the team's objective and then ask questions
related to any concerns or challenges that he or she perceives as
obstacles to accomplishing the mission (see pointer).

Only when there has been open discussion of the objective will
the team members be able to fully commit themselves to it. Someone should record the team's concerns so that the stakeholder can
respond appropriately to any of the issues beyond the control of
the team. These issues can include setting boundaries for areas not
within the team's purview, the budget and resource availability, time-
frame for completing the project, and so on.

A sample list of questions that the team members can discuss
might include
    ◆ What must the team deliver to be considered successful?
    ◆ How will we measure and track our success?
    ◆ How will we know when the work is completed?

Quick Exercise to Clarify Your Team Mission

◆ Hand out an index card to all team members and have them write down the mission of the team using plain script. Be sure they do not include their names on the card.

◆ Randomly redistribute the cards to the group. Ask that they respect each other's privacy and not try to discern handwriting or the author of each mission. Confirm this understanding by asking for questions.

◆ Go around the room and have each team member read the mission listed on the card.

◆ Document verbatim all responses on a flipchart or white board.

◆ Hold a quick election to vote on the mission that the group believes is most accurate.

◆ Ask why they believe the winning vote is best choice.

◆ Have the full team mission prepared on sheets for the entire group and distribute after the discussion. Discuss any gaps they see between the winning mission and the actual mission.

◆ Ask if the team's vote was accurate.

◆ Clarify the correct mission fully with your team. Ask for questions to help reinforce the team's objectives.

2.   Low Trust Levels Among Team Members

As mentioned earlier in this book, a lack of trust is one of the most pervasive problems on any team. According to authors Steven L. Phillips and Robin L. Elledge (1994) in their book, *Team Building for the Future—Beyond the Basics*, "Both acts of commission (doing something) and acts of omission (not doing something) can lead to mistrust. In fact, the most common factors cited for a lack of trust within a team are the routine and inadvertently executed misdeeds all of us are guilty of from time to time." They cite four common areas of behavior that contribute to mistrust among team members:

◆ Unpredictable behavior—mood swings or constant changes in deadlines or expectations for outcomes.

◆ Broken commitments—failure to keep even small commitments.

◆ Unclear communications—vague directions, changes in communication, or miscommunication.

◆ Lack of openness—perceptions of controlling behavior, vague or politically motivated communications.

The antidote for this problem is generally found in improving communications. Great teams practice open communications without any signs of personal attacks. They pay attention to the little details to recognize each other's contributions and distinctive personalities. Constructive criticism is always respectful and is geared toward clarifying information for the team.

Small, frequent team building exercises at the start of the project help team members get to know each other, begin to build trust, and reduce or avoid these tensions.

Periodically, the most successful teams revisit their rules for team engagement. This helps all members to recognize when their behavior may have slipped out of alignment with that of the rest of the team. Many teams institute a group assessment and rate themselves on their progress to date as well as their ability to listen and support each other as agreed on at the start of the team process.

3. Poor Team Communication Skills

Strong teams have a lot of discussion and use active listening and
e on the team participates—as if in a round robin ap-
Members listen to each other and ask for clarification to ex-
eir shared pool of understanding during the discussion.

Questions That Improve Team Conversations

◆ What is the value of effective listening skills and how would that help us?

◆ What would open communication look like?

◆ What can we do to help each other ensure that all are contributing equally in the discussion?

◆ What do we agree to do if discussions appear to get off track?

Every idea is listened to. Questions are asked in very respectful ways and members draw together points made by other members to enhance the discussion. Members discuss their fears openly and note when they are feeling uncomfortable with any topic. If the discussion gets off the track, someone brings it back in a respectful way. Even when there is disagreement, team members acknowledge how and when they can agree or disagree and the team is comfortable with noting that they may have to return to this topic at a future point. They do not seek to avoid conflict but acknowledge their differences openly.

When assignments are given or decisions are made, a summary of assignments and decisions is reviewed at the end of the meeting to ensure all members are aware of their responsibilities.

For Team Leaders

Have a dominator?

A dominator is someone who always likes to talk. Set a three-minute rule, introduce the topic, and allow everyone else a turn in a round robin fashion. Announce when time is up and move to the next individual.

STEP 9

Addressing Conflict

◆ Be on alert—listen for trouble.

◆ Address conflict immediately.

◆ Do not give negative feedback electronically—
   make this a team rule—only provide negative
   feedback in person or over the phone, if
   absolutely necessary.

4. Poor Handling of Team Conflicts

Basic conflicts among team members arise for a variety of reasons. To deal with conflict effectively, it is important that the team leader recognize the nature and source of the problem. Dealing with an emotional issue like feelings of rejection, scorn, or defensiveness is very different than correcting a lack of consensus on the team or the methods to use to address a problem. Substantive issues, however, can often generate emotional reactions so be sure to separate the issue from the emotion.

As a general rule, always deal with the emotional content of the issues first. It is impossible for a team member to have an open discussion on the rational issue until he or she has adequately cleared and vented the strong emotions that may have arisen during an encounter in a meeting. Our bodies are naturally designed to react to any perceived danger by closing down the rational problem-solving sections of the brain so that blood can be diverted to the extremities to "fight or take flight."

It is the team leader's role to recognize and effectively deal with conflicts that arise among team members. Unfortunately, we often fail to address the underlying emotional issues involved between team members because we are poorly trained to handle emotions. It is human nature to back away from such risky conversations and stick only to the safe side of substantive issues. The good news is that it doesn't have to be that way. As the authors

Kerry Patterson, Joseph Grenny, Ron McMillan, and Al Switzler wrote in their masterful book, *Crucial Conversations,* leaders who recognize when the conversation has turned counterproductive and work to rebuild safety on the team can readily resolve conflicts before they render the entire team dysfunctional (2002).

The techniques listed here suggest that team members slow down and recognize how they are responding to this perceived conflict. Some members will become verbally aggressive, whereas others will resort to silence and retreat from the discussion. The skilled team leader can ask both parties to acknowledge their feelings and identify the assumptions they made that caused the conflicting situation. Then, the leader can help them process a "mutual purpose" and brainstorm new strategies for achieving this purpose.

5. Poor Team Process

Organizations that foster great team processes understand the need to invest time and resources to properly set up the

STEP 9

team. Many teams start out with an extended team kick-off meeting during which the groundwork for team communication, trust, and processes is laid. The foundation of a great team includes these elements:

◆ **Get to know each other.** Find out about each member's background, skills, personal strengths, and challenges. This is a great time for team building exercises and personality assessment tools to identify individual preferences for communication, decision making, organization, and so on.

◆ **Have a mission and a plan.** This is also the time to review the team mission and get a clear picture of its meaning for each team member. Also, those involved need to know what the team project plan is and the time frame for completing the project.

◆ **Determine how the team will work together.** This is the time to set team ground rules such as attendance, starting/quitting on time, setting and following an agenda, note-taking responsibilities, how to deal with conflicts, participation, communication and discussion courtesy, confidentiality, work assignments, and so forth.

◆ **Figure out how decisions will be made.** Decide the steps required to make decisions, what vital information will be needed to make the decision, who is affected, who will have responsibility for ultimately making the decision, and so on. Also, the team needs to understand whether decisions will be made by one person, by group consensus, by a subgroup, or through a voting process.

◆ **Build skills.** Team members may need training in how to collect information, how to work on interviewing skills, stakeholder involvement, project planning, specific methods to use to achieve an end result, and other applicable tools or techniques.

6.   Strong Senior-Management Sponsorship

The role of the senior-level sponsor or stakeholder is to help define, oversee, and provide support to the team. Without ongoing senior sponsorship, team initiatives can falter. Sometimes

People Game

Here's an idea to encourage people to read the information posted about their colleagues prior to your kick-off meeting. Invite them to play a game in which they match their colleagues' names to some trivia about them.

Purpose: Gives team members a means for starting to get to know each other and to begin to build interpersonal relationships before the start of the meeting.

Setup: First, collect trivia about your teammates, ask them for little-known information about themselves. Second, create a numbered list containing this information. Include space next to each line that provides enough room for someone to write in a name.

How to Play: Print and distribute (or email) the list to all team members prior to the meeting. Ask them to match a person's name to each trivia question on the sheet, and to bring completed sheets to the meeting. Draw prizes for those who submit completed sheets.

Debrief: Be explicit—explain to the team, right from the start, that getting to know each other and becoming comfortable working together is critical to the success of the team, and that you're willing not only to support this behavior, but also to model it.

STEP 9

improvement efforts bubble up from employee groups, but without ultimate sponsorship from a senior-level manager, there is a risk that the improvement team cannot sustain and secure resources to complete the process. A sponsor does more than just speak at the project kick-off meeting. When a team encounters resistance from other areas of the organization, the senior sponsor goes to bat for the team's efforts. The sponsor can also play a vital role in providing guidance and direction for the team project and also ensures alignment with other corporate initiatives. The sponsor looks for updates and shows evidence of reading them. He or she reinforces progress and offers help in areas that need it. The sponsor helps blast through roadblocks and supports the team leader. The sponsor provides quiet, background support as well as visible support.

7. Lack of Accountability Among Team Members

The success of the team hinges on team members completing assigned project tasks. When team members fail to complete assignments by the assigned deadlines, the team leader needs to assess the root cause of these failures. Are they the result of

- ◆ **Lack of training or skill?** Help team members understand various aspects of data analysis, project planning, presentation skills, and so on.
- ◆ **Lack of understanding?** Invite subject matter experts to attend team meetings to explain technical issues or to assist in clarifying perceived barriers.
- ◆ **Lapse in memory?** Review the team's ground rules and clarify the roles and responsibilities of team members.
- ◆ **Something else?** Meet privately with members who don't complete assignments on time.

One additional suggestion is to treat each problem as a "group process problem"—even if it is a problem that only one or two members have. This strategy can have a cross-training effect on the group and also brings in various viewpoints to potential problems.

8. Team Is Overwhelmed By Work

The team leader is responsible for managing the team's work process and for assessing and intervening when team members become overwhelmed with too much work or too many projects. When the team leader senses that the energy and behavior on the team have become frenetic or chaotic, it is time to revisit the team's priorities. Signals of frenzy or chaos include

◆ The ongoing talk among team members includes frequent statements like, "There is no way I can accomplish this project by this deadline along with all the other things I have on my plate."

◆ Assignments are missing or late.

◆ Communication grinds to a halt.

◆ Members are irritable or hostile and have short fuses.

Consider holding a "Time Out to Refresh" team meeting. In this session, everyone on the team identifies all the projects or tasks he or she is responsible for. Then the leader and the team help each member identify a limited number of high-priority projects with an assigned deadline that the member will be held accountable for. This approach provides a relief valve in that it helps team members focus on the real priority issues, and it also releases some of the pressure of being overwhelmed because the team member will not be required to complete the other, less significant tasks until some later, defined time. This process also helps to set up additional team activities that benefit team members:

◆ Team members develop ideas on ways to help each other find additional resources or remove perceived barriers in the organization to complete projects.

◆ Participants will understand the ramifications of their decisions and make difficult choices about priorities.

◆ Team members will hold themselves accountable for establishing detailed project plans so they can accomplish their projects according to established deadlines.

It's always a good practice for the team leader to meet with individual team members outside of the regular meetings to coach them on identifying lead times for project steps, overcoming roadblocks, and other problem-solving topics.

STEP **9**

9. Wrong People on the Team

The most successful teams are equally concerned with how well the job gets done as well as getting the job done. Consequently, it is important to ensure that the team consists of people who have the right cross-functional technical/work experience with the project's subject matter. Members should be drawn from various ranks within the organization (most likely excluding management representatives who might unduly influence or intimidate team members).

Ideally, team members should be people who are considered informal leaders in their areas and who are respected by others in their departments. It is always good to include members who are interested in working collaboratively, who are open to new ideas, and who are concerned with the improvement process and/or have a stake in the outcome. Additionally, members should be people who have expertise in one or more areas of process improvement, problem solving, data collection and analysis, customer service, documentation, and so forth.

Team members should also be considered based on a good fit with other members, taking in complementary personalities and people who will challenge each other to stretch beyond their comfort levels.

Some teams are already formed. With those teams, value the various perspectives that exist. If you find a lot of similar personality styles, bring in different views when appropriate.

10. Team Is Too Quick to Find Solutions

Sometimes team members with the best of intentions want to solve technical issues with "quick fixes." These "fix-it listeners" tend to want to patch the symptoms rather than find the root of the problem. Too often, these team members can influence the team into making hasty decisions before the proper analysis has been completed.

Team leaders need to be patient in their team-training process and emphasize the value of the scientific approach to investigating and analyzing the issues fully before attempting to find solutions. The team leader should refer the team members back to the team charter and ground rules for working through the entire process. Sometimes the team leader needs to take the "fix-it" member aside and point out the consequences of moving ahead too quickly.

Remember, not all conflict is bad. Conflict can serve as a stimulus to energize team members to think more fully through assumptions and help members think outside the box. This is how teams achieve alignment. It is important to recognize the signals among team members that the discussion is becoming overly sensitive. When this happens the team leader needs to acknowledge the sensitivity of the discussion and slow down the pace of the discussion to explore how members are feeling and what their assumptions are concerning this sensitive area. A high-functioning team leader can set the tone for encouraging everyone to question what she or he knows and to develop a common understanding or shared pool of meaning among the members.

Group Problem Solving

There are advantages and disadvantages to group problem solving. Certainly sometimes it is easier for one person to sit down and figure out what needs to be done. The advantage of working with a team is that different people are seeing the issue from different sides. Input from others can be helpful in coming up with the most complete solution.

Figure 9.1 shows a problem-solving model that works well for teams. This model will work while solving problems within the team as well as using the process to solve obstacles when achieving the team's goals or mission. How does this work? You may need to do some research and investigation to really define the problem. Once defined, the team can generate ideas and identify possible solutions to the problem. From those possible solutions, select the

FIGURE 9.1
Problem-Solving Model for Teams

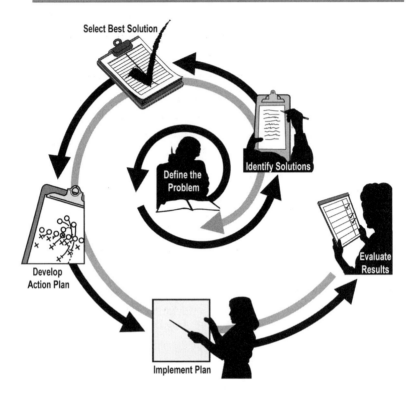

- ◆ Research and define the problem
  - ◆ Generate ideas and identify possible solutions
    - ◆ Select the best solution
      - ◆ Develop action plan
        - ◆ Implement plan
          - ◆ Evaluate results against desired outcome

best solution—the one that will best address the defined problem. Next you will develop action plans to enact the solution and implement those plans.

STEP **9**

Many times the problem-solving process ends here. I recommend that once action plans have been implemented that the team examines whether the outcome is what you were looking for. Did it solve the problem? Was the problem properly defined? If it is not what you were looking or hoping for, you may need to go back into the process and ensure the problem was defined properly, see if another solution is better, determine if the plans created were implemented properly. Sometimes it takes more than one attempt to solve a problem or accomplish a goal. And sometimes the lessons learned along the way are valuable.

There can be a number of areas to watch out for in a problem-solving cycle. Table 9.1 shows what can happen if you spend too much or too little time in any one area.

Make It Happen!

Solving problems will be a part of every team experience. If there weren't things to figure out and be accomplished, you wouldn't need a team, right? How those difficulties are dealt with can help to strengthen the team or can cause resentments. Helping each other to maneuver through difficulties and solve problems can be a very helpful experience for team members and can increase the results achieved by the team.

STEP **9**

TABLE 9.1

Trouble with Steps in Problem-Solving Process

The Step	If Cut Short You May . . .	Too Much Time Spent Here Can Cause . . .
Research and define the problem	Make assumptions and not properly identify the problem	Analysis paralysis—the frustrated team members may lose momentum
Generate ideas and identify possible solutions	Grab the first idea and miss a better idea	So many ideas are generated it becomes difficult to synthesize them
Select the best solution	Spend too much time or money solving the problem	Time spent finding the "perfect" solution, when you just need a great one
Develop action plan	Create "Swiss cheese plan"—there may be holes in it	The action plan is more complex than it needs to be—shoot for efficiency combined with quality
Implement plan	Have voids or overlapping effort	Process can take longer than it needs to; team can spend time on effort that doesn't add value
Evaluate	Not realize that your efforts didn't really address the right problem	Lost time that could have been better spent on a different task

STEP 9

Reward and Celebrate Success

Uncover what is important to each team member. That is what will motivate them to do their best.

—Julie Jacques

My friend Lisa was working virtually on a team as a Level 2 Help Desk resource. She found communication to be difficult; often she did not get what she needed. She would participate in regular meetings with the team, but the manager didn't reach out to her. There was never any feedback—either positive or constructive. No one even acknowledged that work was getting done.

At the end of a status meeting, the manager wrapped things up and announced that this would be Lisa's last team meeting with them. It was an announcement. No goodbye, no thanks for the work, no job well done, no acknowledgment of her contributions—no nothing. Lisa had worked full time for six months with absolutely no acknowledgement of the work she had done or what she had contributed to the team. And no one even said goodbye. The manager was very comfortable with the technical piece of his job. But he was not addressing the feelings of the people on the team.

STEP **10**

Importance of Recognition

Quite often, people on project teams have a full-time job and then the team responsibilities on top of that. Recognizing the additional effort a team member gives is important. Recognition and rewards (small or large) can help motivate performance. People are willing to put in extra effort when someone notices and appreciates their contributions.

Here is an example: I worked on a large project once for a VP of Sales. To complete this project required the input of many people in the organization, but it was my responsibility and it was on my performance plan. I worked hard collecting, coordinating, and integrating all of the pieces. I made sure to thank all the contributors for their help. I completed the project on time and put it on my boss's desk. Then I waited. When I didn't hear anything, I was deflated! He didn't even look at my work! It wasn't until some time later, in front of 100 sales people that I heard him compliment it. I was grateful for the recognition but was shocked at the timing and lack of feedback earlier. What I learned: When people do something good, notice it right away!

POINTER

Nothing else can quite substitute for a few well-chosen, well-timed, sincere words of praise. They are absolutely free—and worth a fortune.

—*Sam Walton, founder of Wal-Mart*

Why do some people fail to recognize efforts? Do they think once they acknowledge a good job, they will need to keep praising everyone? Is it because other teams will then wonder why they aren't being recognized? Are the team members simply doing what you told them to do, which *is* their job, so why bother to say anything more? I think most people would agree that motivation has its place and turnover is costly. So, there is little cost to recognize and sometimes an even greater cost *not* to recognize people's efforts.

STEP **10**

Types of Recognition

Everyone knows a pay raise or bonus check is motivating to many people. In these times of budget cuts and economic uncertainty, raises and bonuses may be nonexistent. But there are other ways to reward and motivate teams that may be more affordable. Consider offering these reward ideas:

◆ certificate for dinner out with a spouse or friend
◆ gift cards
◆ a group lunch
◆ a celebration event at the completion of a project
◆ time off (going out to lunch and then letting everyone go home early or giving them a day off)
◆ a gift for the office that recognizes the individual's effort (special clock, something for the wall)
◆ movie passes or tickets to an event
◆ recognition in front of the group (although this appeals to many people, be sure to be as specific as possible about the contributions made; not all cultures appreciate this).

But what if there is no money available for gifts? What if your budget is such that you can't even find $50 to take people out to lunch? Or, what if you are not the team leader? There are plenty of ways to show people how much their efforts are appreciated that don't involve an expenditure of funds. Try these ideas:

◆ Have a one–on–one conversation with the individual's manager. Tell the manager about the team member's hard work, expertise, and value to the team. Make the contribution clear to the manager.
◆ Provide input/mention into the team member's annual performance appraisal.
◆ Provide visibility upward. Let upper management know of the individual team member's contribution. Or, ask a high-level manager to come to a meeting to see the contribution being made firsthand.
◆ Provide visibility cross-functionally. If someone's ultimate goal is to get into the marketing department, make sure the individual has access and visibility to that department.

STEP **10**

- Make the team effort developmental and career assisting. If there is something a member wants to learn, help him or her do that. Let this experience prepare the team member for the next step.
- Write a note by hand, showing appreciation or recognizing achievement.
- Give certificates of recognition or appreciation that can be displayed in the workspace.
- Provide time off work (a morning, an afternoon, or a day).

These small gestures cost little or nothing, but their payoff can be enormous. When delivering praise or positive feedback, do not sandwich it between a list of To-Dos. If the contribution has been meaningful, to get the full effect, praise and thanks should be delivered personally and as a singular act.

Things to Consider When Rewarding Success

If you have multiple generations on your team, find out what the various age groups find motivating and rewarding. Recognition won't necessarily be a one-size-fits-all affair.

GenX, GenY folks may want feedback or rewards quickly, as events occur. Recognize their accomplishments so others see them in a positive light. Rewarding them with time off and respecting their free time will likely be a good thing. These individuals may appreciate development opportunities. Also, giving them a chance to mentor and teach others may be seen as a growth opportunity.

For **boomers**, cash, an event, or something tangible (gift cards, tickets) will likely be appreciated. They like to be acknowledged as leaders. Show how their contribution affects the organization.

Different cultures and global locales can also help determine the kind of reward that makes sense. If you are offering bagels and

10 Characteristics of Companies That Care

- Sustain a work environment founded on dignity and respect for all employees.
- Make employees feel their jobs are important.
- Cultivate the full potential of all employees.
- Encourage individual pursuit of work/life balance.
- Enable the well-being of individuals and their families through compensation, benefits, policies, and practices.
- At all levels, develop great leaders who excel at managing people as well as results.
- Appreciate and recognize the contributions of people who work for the company.
- Establish and communicate standards for ethical behavior and integrity.
- Get involved in community endeavors and/or public policy.
- Consider the human toll when making business decisions.

Source: From Center for Companies That Care.

coffee at the meeting in the office, send a Starbucks card to a member in another location. Some cultures are not used to being thanked or recognized for work accomplished. They consider it their job.

Companies That Care

Companies that care prize employees and are committed to community service. To sustain their values, these companies consistently demonstrate them in the work environment. These characteristics define the standard for all organizations desiring to be recognized as caring, responsible organizations.

STEP **10**

Although these characteristics are written for a company, they have team relevance as well. Here are some ways to use the same ideas to create a culture that celebrates success:

- **Budget for an off-site gathering.** If possible, include family or significant others.
- **Develop awards recognizing individuals and teams who make a significant contribution to the project.** The impact can involve diversity, innovation, service and charitable activities, cost savings, leadership, and other efforts important to the business and/or team culture.
- **Create an award for specific types of contributions.** For example, recognize technical advancements and achievements by teams.
- **Distribute ABCD awards.** When effort goes "Above and Beyond the Call of Duty," make available preprinted thank-you notes that any team member can give to another team member in recognition of an extra effort or for simply doing something nice.
- **Provide rewards or incentives for cross-training and learning other jobs for the benefit of the team.**
- **Give on-the-spot awards** for team members who exceed expectations.
- **Invite team members** to give positive recognition to each other during team meetings.
- **Share the kudos.** Many times there are people or departments outside of the team that contribute to success. Let everyone know that. Thank them and let their bosses know. Once that is the culture you create, the next time you ask for something individuals will willingly participate. Don't just recognize the same team members all the time. It is de-motivating for the rest of the team.
- **Be sensitive to cultural considerations regarding recognition.** Public recognition is great for many, but some people and some cultures aren't comfortable being recognized in front of their peers. Ask first.
- **Provide a traveling trophy** to show recognition for milestone efforts or results that exceed expectations.

◆ **Promote visibility.** Thank people's efforts by "carbon copying" upper management.

◆ **Offer recognition in performance reviews** in the form of promotions and pay increases.

Can Recognition Backfire?

Isn't all recognition meant to celebrate team or individual success? Aren't all rewards and gifts welcome? Not so, particularly if thought is not given to individuals' preferences.

Let's say you're the team leader and give the team holiday turkeys as a thank-you for getting through a particularly demanding stage of the project. They are

STEP 10

frozen turkeys. You made a big presentation, recognizing the extra efforts and saying thank you. Everyone seems appreciative. But here is what you don't see. One of the team members commutes to work on a train. Tonight she has plans after work. So, is she going to carry a 15-pound turkey around all evening? The answer is no. Oh, by the way, she is single, she doesn't need a 15-pound turkey, and she doesn't like turkey anyway. She ends up giving her "recognition" to someone else. The intention is good, but needs to be clearly thought through.

To keep recognition, rewards, and simple thank-yous from backfiring, follow these tips:

POINTER

For Team Members

Anyone can recognize and "reward" positive contributions to the team. Sometimes a positive comment from a team member goes further than recognition from the team leader or project sponsor.

◆ **Be consistent.** Consistency is vital. Create a culture of recognition and let people know what they do has value. If you start and then stop, you will have partial success. Don't praise so much that recognition becomes expected, but do it enough to show that you care and notice. Recognize the big milestones along the way, not just at the end.

◆ **Be specific.** Saying "Great job!" is not specific. Tell the person what was good and why it was important.

◆ **Know your team members.** Ask what they like and write it down so you remember; show appreciation appropriately.

◆ **Be prompt.** Celebrate accomplishments as soon after they occur as possible and use that as impetus to move on to the next goal or milestone.

◆ **Keep the reward in line with contribution.** Not all team members contribute equally—people's roles are different. Based on a person's role, her or his major contribution may be up front or at the end of the project. Or it may be a small amount contributed all along the way. Good rewards are in step with the contribution.

Learning how your team would like to be recognized—and how you can show your appreciation—is a vital step toward making sure that your efforts will be appropriate.

Make It Happen!

When you think about all that teams contribute to the organization, making plans for recognizing good work just makes sense. It also makes sense to put some incentives behind cost-saving initiatives, doesn't it? Consider using a portion of the cost savings earned for a team celebration and rewards while the company continues to reap the benefits of those savings over the next several years.

Have you ever noticed that the absence of thanks and recognition are very de-motivating? A lack of appreciation makes it seem that no one is aware of all of the hard work that gets done. When it appears that no one takes the time to recognize good work and over-the-top contributions, employees tend to lose interest in their work. They may become disillusioned and can even look for other job opportunities. Building a culture that celebrates success in the form of rewards, recognition, and just saying "thank you" keeps motivation, enthusiasm, and activity high.

Be sure that when you celebrate, the sentiments offered are personal and sincere. Thanks or appreciation from the team leader, sponsor, or another leader in the organization can go a long way. A small token of recognition becomes more meaningful with a personalized, handwritten note instead of a blanket email.

STEP **10**

NOTES:

_____

_____

_____

_____

_____

_____

_____

_____

_____

_____

_____

_____

_____

_____

_____

_____

_____

_____

_____

_____

APPENDIX A: STEP ONE TOOLS

Kick-off Meeting Process/Activities

- Prepare a guide for email etiquette.
- Identify the percentage of available work time that each person will devote to the project.
- Identify the relationship of the project to other priorities and responsibilities.
- Establish the percentage of time expected for billable work and administrative work (it is unrealistic to expect more billable hours than 80 percent of capacity, particularly if the job requires intense concentration or creativity).
- Work with team members to define the methodology for measuring success (ideally, team members define their own performance metrics).

Sample Kick-Off Meeting Agenda

- Describe the vision for the project.
- Conduct team member introductions.
- Provide context for how the team and the project fits into the overall organization and its strategy.
- Provide a project overview.
- Review roles and responsibilities.
- Conduct team building activities.
- Review team charter / ground rules / rules of engagement / guidelines for team interaction.
- Define the communication paths among team members; with upper management, with functional groups, with customers, and with other employees.
- Discuss project expectations—both yours and theirs.
- Discuss project assumptions.

- Define behavioral expectations (e.g., time, decision-making processes, conflict management, escalation pathways, reward and recognition, and so on).
- Ensure everyone understands the project objectives, scope, purpose, as well as roles and responsibilities.
- Test collaborative software access and settings.
- Conduct collaboration, tool orientation / training.
- Assign specific action items, due dates, and dependencies to team members.
- Help team establish both formal and informal communication channels.
- Identify dates/times for status meetings.
- Establish a tentative date for the next milestone meeting.

Setting the Team's Ground Rules

The first process to develop with any new team should always be establishing team ground rules. These rules will help all team members know what the parameters are in getting things done. Keep in mind that ground rules should not be written in advance by the team leader; the rules must be developed by the team, agreed on by everyone, and ultimately followed. Here is an example of a few ground rules that work for almost every team:

Our Team's Ground Rules
- We are committed to working passionately toward our team mission.
- Everyone on our team actively participates.
- All ideas are welcome—there are no bad ideas.
- We recognize that every team member brings value to the team.
- The team will strive to listen, will not interrupt others who are speaking, and will minimize dominating discussions.
- We respect the opinions of others.
- The team always tests assumptions.
- We realize that at times we will disagree.
- We will keep distractions to a minimum.

- All decisions are made by group consensus.
- All discussion within our group is confidential—this is a safe place.
- Ideas are owned by the team and not by individuals.
- We will enjoy the team process.

Build the ground rules of the team together.

A P P E N D I X   B:
S T E P   T H R E E   T O O L S

Sample Team Communication Plan

What	With Whom	Who's Responsible?	Purpose	When	Type/ Method
Initial Stake-holder meeting: Regional directors	Regional directors: Nick Gauss, Diane Boewe	Team members meet with regional directors regarding event planning. Review organizational rules and guidelines to ensure program meets criteria.	Team Lead	Jan. 7, 2010	Face-to-face meeting at Aurora Office
Initial Stake-holder meeting: Corporate sponsors	Corporate Sponsors: XYZ Company, ACME	Team Lead	Secure donations through presentation of the project and positive impact on corporate sponsor. Present business case for financial support.	April 5, 2010– April 12, 2010	Individual face-to-face meeting at downtown Chicago ACME office

Sample Team Communication Plan

Project Name: _____ Date: _____

Timing	Deliverable	Description	Delivery Method	Target Audience	Frequency	Owner	Approval(s)	Business or PM Responsibilities	Status
January Key focus New project timeline	Updated project timeline	Inform all stakeholders and project team members of updated project timeline	Email Meetings SharePoint	All	On-time update	Project manager	Business sponsor	<Update>	Draft review
	<Deliverable>	Description	<Delivery Method>	<Audience>	<Frequency>	<Owner>	<Recipient>	<Update>	<Update>
	<Deliverable>	Description	<Delivery Method>	<Audience>	<Frequency>	<Owner>	<Recipient>	<Update>	<Update>
	<Deliverable>	Description	<Delivery Method>	<Audience>	<Frequency>	<Owner>	<Recipient>	<Update>	<Update>
Week 2	<Deliverable>	Description	<Delivery Method>	<Audience>	<Frequency>	<Owner>	<Recipient>	<Update>	<Update>
	<Deliverable>	Description	<Delivery Method>	<Audience>	<Frequency>	<Owner>	<Recipient>	<Update>	<Update>
	<Deliverable>	Description	<Delivery Method>	<Audience>	<Frequency>	<Owner>	<Recipient>	<Update>	<Update>
	<Deliverable>	Descript on	<Delivery Method>	<Audience>	<Frequency>	<Owner>	<Recipient>	<Update>	<Update>
Week 3	<Deliverable>	Description	<Delivery Method>	<Audience>	<Frequency>	<Owner>	<Recipient>	<Update>	<Update>
Week 4	<Deliverable>	Description	<Delivery Method>	<Audience>	<Frequency>	<Owner>	<Recipient>	<Update>	<Update>

APPENDIX C:
STEP FIVE TOOLS

Team Exercise (to emphasize the importance of following prescribed processes)

This activity, created by Lanie Jordan, draws a parallel between a cooking recipe and following a process. It emphasizes the importance of following the team's processes.

◆ Distribute the Recipe Exercise (Mrs. Ryan's Mac & Cheese). Allow teammates five minutes to answer the question.

◆ Ask for answers to the question: What do goals and recipes have in common?

◆ Facilitate a discussion about the benefits and advantages of having defined processes.

◆ Ask what happens when you don't follow the recipe? What can happen to us if we don't follow the process?

Mrs. Ryan's Mac & Cheese

Ingredients

- cooking spray
- $1^1/_2$ lbs of grated extra sharp cheddar cheese
- $1/_4$ lb of grated Pennsylvania Swiss cheese
- 5 cups dried elbow pasta
- 3 tablespoons butter
- $1/_2$ cup milk
- $1/_4$ cup plain breadcrumbs (optional)

Directions

Coat a large casserole dish with cooking spray. Boil elbow pasta and drain. Wipe out pot and place back on the stove. Melt 3 tablespoons of butter over low to medium heat. Add cooked pasta to the melted butter in the pot. Combine both types of cheese in with your mixture. Warm your milk slightly in the microwave for approximately 30 seconds (depending on your microwave settings). Add warmed milk slowly to the mixture as you stir. Continue stirring until all the cheese is melted thoroughly into the pasta.

Preheat your oven to 375 degrees. Transfer all the contents into your sprayed casserole dish. Cook for 20 to 25 minutes until bubbly and slightly browned on top, checking often during the last five minutes. Let stand for 5 to 10 minutes. Bon Appétit!

What Do Recipes and Goals Have in Common?

1. _____

2. _____

3. _____

4. _____

5. _____

6. _____

7. _____

APPENDIX D: STEP EIGHT TOOLS

PowerPoint Tips for Online Meetings

Here is a list of surefire PowerPoint presentation tips and techniques to help make your virtual meetings a success:

- ◆ **Readability is key**—Make sure the font is large enough for everyone to see. Another tip to remember is that too many words can make following along a burden for the audience. People will soon lose interest.
- ◆ **Stick to main points**—Only put the key points of the presentation on your PowerPoint slides. You can avoid the monotony of having your presentation verbatim on each slide.
- ◆ **Use clear titles**—Each slide needs to have a clear title summarizing its purpose. Using a large, bolder font can help ensure the title stands out from the rest of the slide.
- ◆ **Use simple backgrounds**—Pay attention to your color selections. Also, make sure the background does not detract from the words or diagrams. If you choose colors that are too dark or patterns that are too bold, chances are the slides will be difficult to read.
- ◆ **Use graphs and diagrams**—Using visual images like graphs and diagrams can really help make a point. Images also break up the presentation and provide some visual interest.

Team Building for Virtual Teams or Co-located Teams

Team building activities can be simple or extravagant. The following icebreaker, written by Brian Cole Miller, author of *More Quick Team-Building Activities for Busy Managers*, gives team members an easy and light-hearted way to introduce themselves and divulge a small bit of personal information.

Purpose: To introduce members of a team. Good when the team members don't know each other well or you want them to warm up to each other.

Activity: Team members introduce themselves by playing their cell phone ring tones.

Tip: Not everyone will know how to play his/her ring tone, so be prepared to call team members' phones to make their phones ring.

How it works:
1. Explain the activity to the team. Tell them what is entailed and why you are doing it.
2. Have each participant introduce him/herself with job-relevant information like name, position, location, department, and so on.
3. Then have each participant play his/her cell phone ring tone and explain why he/she picked that one. This will prompt people to reveal a tiny bit about their personal lives.

Questions to ask:
- Why did you choose that ring tone?
- Do you have special ring tones for individuals or specific numbers?
- When do you put your phone on vibrate? When do you turn it off completely?
- What other steps can we take to get to know each other on the job?

Virtual Teams Glossary

Wikipedia Terms and Definitions

Term	Definition
Aggregation/ Aggregator	A collection of web feeds accessible in one spot is known as aggregation, which is performed by an Internet aggregator.
Atom Syndication Format (Atom)	A format based on XML used to deliver web feeds (news feeds). Atom was created in competition with RSS.
Blog	A blog (a contraction of the term "web log") is a website usually maintained by an individual who posts regular entries: commentary, descriptions of events, or other material such as graphics or video. Entries are commonly displayed in reverse-chronological order. "Blog" can also be used as a verb, meaning to maintain or add content to a blog.
Crowd-sourcing	Crowdsourcing is a neologism for the act of taking a task traditionally performed by an employee or contractor, and outsourcing it to an undefined, generally large group of people, in the form of an open call.
Facebook	Facebook is a popular, free-access social networking website that is operated and privately owned by Facebook, Inc. Users can join networks organized by city, workplace, school, and region to connect and interact with other people. You can also add friends and send them messages as well as update your personal profile to notify friends about what you are doing.
Instant Message (IM)	Instant messaging (IM) uses technologies that create real-time text-based communication between/among two or more participants over the Internet or some form of internal network/intranet.
LinkedIn	LinkedIn is a business-oriented social networking site founded in December 2002 and launched in May 2003 used mainly for professional networking. As of October 2008, it had more than 30 million registered users spanning 150 industries.

Mashup	A web application that combines data and/or functionality from more than one source.
Micro-blogging	A form of multimedia blogging that allows users to send brief text updates (say, 140 characters or fewer) or micromedia such as photos or audio clips and publish them, either to be viewed by anyone or by a restricted group chosen by the user. These messages can be submitted in a variety of ways, including text messaging, instant messaging, email, MP3, or the web. The content of a micro-blog differs from a traditional blog in that it is typically more topical, smaller in aggregate file size (e.g., text, audio, or video) but is the same in that people use it for both business and personal reasons. Many micro-blogs provide this short commentary on a person-to-person level or share news about a company's products and services.
MySpace	A social networking website with an interactive, user-submitted network of friends, personal profiles, blogs, groups, photos, music, and videos for teenagers and adults internationally.
Ning	An online platform enabling users to create their own social websites and social networks, launched in October 2005.
PDA (Personal Data Assistant)	A handheld computer that is also known as a palmtop computer. Newer PDAs also have both color screens and audio capabilities, enabling them to be used as mobile phones, (smartphones), web browsers, or portable media players. Many PDAs can access the Internet, intranets, or extranets via Wi-Fi or Wireless Wide-Area Networks (WWANs).
Podcast	A podcast is a series of audio or video digital-media files that are distributed over the Internet by syndicated download, through web feeds, to portable media players and personal computers. Though the same content may also be made available by direct download or streaming, a podcast is distinguished from other digital-media formats by its ability to be syndicated, subscribed to, and downloaded automatically when new content is added. Like the term "broadcast," podcast can refer either to the series of content itself or to the method by which it is syndicated; the latter is also called podcasting. The host or author of a podcast is often called a podcaster.

RSS (Really Simple Syndication)	A family of web feed formats used to publish frequently updated works in a standardized format, e.g., blogs, audio, and video. RSS feeds can be read using an RSS reader. An XML file format allows the information to be published once and viewed by many different programs.
SMS (Short Message Service)	A communications protocol allowing the interchange of short text messages between mobile telephone devices.
Social Networks	A social structure made of nodes (which are generally individuals or organizations) that are tied by one or more specific type of interdependency such as values, visions, ideas, financial exchange, friendship, kinship, dislike, conflict, or trade. The resulting graph-based structures are often very complex.
Social Software	Social software encompasses a range of software systems that allow users to interact and share data. This computer-mediated communication has become very popular with social sites like MySpace and Facebook, media sites like Flickr and YouTube, and commercial sites like Amazon.com and eBay. Many of these applications share characteristics like open APIs, service-oriented design, and the ability to upload data and media. The terms "Web 2.0" and (for large-business applications) "Enterprise 2.0" are also used to describe this style of software.
Tag / Word Clouds	A tag cloud or word cloud (or weighted list in visual design) is a visual depiction of user-generated tags or simply the word content of a site, typically used to describe the content of websites. Tags are usually single words and are usually listed alphabetically; the importance of a tag is shown via font size or color. Thus both finding a tag alphabetically or by popularity is possible. The tags are usually hyperlinks that lead to a collection of items that are associated with a tag.
Twitter	A free social networking and micro-blogging service that allows users to send and read other users' updates (otherwise known as tweets), which are text-based posts of up to 140 characters.
Web 2.0	The term "Web 2.0" describes the changing trends in the use of World Wide Web technology and web design that aim to enhance creativity, communications, secure information sharing, collaboration, and functionality of the web. Web 2.0 concepts have led to

Web 2.0 continued	the development and evolution of web culture communities and hosted services, such as social-networking sites, video-sharing sites, wikis, blogs, and folksonomies. The term first became notable after the O'Reilly Media Web 2.0 conference in 2004. Although the term suggests a new version of the World Wide Web, it does not refer to an update to any technical specifications, but rather to changes in the ways software developers and end-users employ the Web.
Web Feed (news feed or syndicated feed)	A web feed (or news feed) is a data format used to provide its users with frequently updated content. Content distributors syndicate a web feed, thereby allowing users to subscribe to it.
Webcams	Video-capturing devices connected to computers or computer networks that often use USB or, if they connect to networks, ethernet or Wi-Fi. They are well known for their low manufacturing costs and flexible applications.
Webinar	Web conference used to conduct live meetings or presentations via the Internet. Each participant sits at his or her own computer and is connected to other participants via the Internet enabled by either a downloaded application or a web-based application in which attendees just type a URL (website address) to enter the conference. "Webinar" is a neologism used to describe a specific type of web conference. It is typically one way, from the speaker to the audience, with limited audience interaction, as in a webcast. A webinar can be collaborative and include polling as well as question-and-answer sessions, allowing full participation between the audience and the presenter. In some cases, the presenter may speak over a standard telephone line, pointing out information being presented on screen, and the audience can respond over their own telephones, preferably a speaker phone.
Wiki	"Wiki, wiki" is Hawaiian for "quick, quick." A wiki is a page or collection of web pages designed to enable anyone who accesses it to contribute or modify content, using a simplified markup language. Wikis are often used to create collaborative websites and to power community websites. The collaborative encyclopedia Wikipedia is one of the best-known wikis. Wikis are used in business to provide intranet and knowledge management systems.

Source: Retrieved from http://en.wikipedia.org.

R E F E R E N C E S

Acuff, J. 2004. *The Relationship Edge in Business*. Hoboken, NJ: Wiley.

Biech, E. 2001. *The Pfeiffer Book of Successful Team Building*. San Francisco: Jossey-Bass/Pfeiffer.

Brown, K., et al. 2006. *Managing Virtual Teams: Getting the Most from Wikis, Blogs and Other Collaborative Tools*. Plano, TX: Wordware Publishing.

Buckingham, M. 2007. *Go Put Your Strengths to Work*. New York: Free Press.

Buckingham, M., and D. Clifton. 2001. *Now Discover Your Strengths*. New York: Free Press.

Buzan, T., and B. Buzan. 1996. *The Mind Map*. New York: Penguin

Caldecott, S., and M. Gelb. 2007. *Innovate Like Edison*. New York: Penguin.

Center for Companies that Care. "Be a Company that Cares." Retrieved December 29, 2008, from http://www.companies-that-care/13_how_1.php

Colocation. Retrieved December 21, 2009, from Wikipedia: http://en.wikipedia.org/wiki/Colocation

Duarte, D., and N. Snyder. 1999. *Mastering Virtual Teams: Strategies, Tools, and Techniques That Succeed*. San Francisco: Jossey-Bass.

EffectiveMeetings.com. "Virtual Team Processes." Retrieved December 29, 2008, from http://www.effectivemeetings.com/technology/virtualteam/virtualte aming.asp.

Elledge, R., and P. Phillips. 1994. *Teambuilding for the Future — Beyond the Basics*. San Diego: Pfeiffer.

Facebook. Retrieved December 29, 2008, from http://www.facebook.com.

Guttman, H.M. 2008. *Great Business Teams Cracking the Code for Standout Performance*. Hoboken, NJ: Wiley.

Haman, G. 2009. *KnowBrainer Tool*. Chicago: SolutionPeople Innovation & Thinkubator.

Harrington-Mack, D. 1994. *The Team Building Tool Kit*. New York: AMACOM.

Katzenback, J., and D. Smith. 2003. *The Wisdom of Teams*. New York: McKinsey & Company.

Kawasaki, G. Blog—"Ten Ways to Use LinkedIn." Retrieved January 4, 2007, from http://blog.guykawasaki.com.

Kostner, J. 1996. *Virtual Leadership: Secrets from the Round Table for the Multi-Site Manager*. New York: Warner Books.

LinkedIn. Retrieved December 29, 2008, from LinkedIn website: http://www.linkedin.com.

Lipnack, J., and J. Stamps. 2000. *Virtual Teams: People Working Across Boundaries with Technology* (2d Edition). New York: Wiley.

Marotta, L. "Top 10 PowerPoint Presentation Tips to Maximize the Effectiveness of Your Online Meetings." Retrieved December 21, 2008, from http://www.web conferencing zone.com/powerpoint-presentation-tips-1.htm.

Miller, B. 2007. *More Quick Team-Building Activities for Busy Managers*. New York: AMACOM.

Mindtools.com. "Rewarding Your Team: Learning Why 'Thank You' Is So Vital." Retrieved from http://www.mindtools.com/pages/article/newTMM_54.htm.

Patterson, K., J. Grenny, R. McMillan, and A. Switzler. 2002. *Crucial Conversations: Tools for Talking When Stakes Are High*. New York: McGraw-Hill.

Rath, T. 2007. *Strengths Finder 2.0*. New York: Gallup Press.

"The Relationship Between Process and Performance on Teams."
Retrieved from http://www.itapintl.com/facultyandresources/
articlelibrarymain/the- relationship-between-process-and-
performance-on-teams.html.

Ross, J. 2006. "Trust Makes the Team Go 'Round." *Harvard
Management Update*, volume 11, number 6, 3–6.

Scholtes, P., B. Joiner, and B. Streibel. 2003. *The Team Handbook*
(3d Edition). Madison, WI: Oriel.

Science Daily. "Working Together in War Rooms Double Teams'
Productivity." Retrieved December 30, 2000, from http://
www.sciencedaily.com/releases/2000/12/001206144705.htm

Second Life. Retrieved December 29, 2008, from http://
www.secondlife.com.

Senge, P. 1990. *The Fifth Discipline*. New York: Doubleday.

Suarez, L. "elsua: The Knowledge Management Blog—Thinking
Outside the Inbox." Retrieved August 21, 2008, from http://
it.toolbox.com/blogs/elsua/the-future-of-work-by-luis-suarez-
full-version-26767.

Twitter. Retrieved December 29, 2008, from http://
www.twitter.com.

Wardell, C. 1998. "The Art of Managing Virtual Teams: Eight Key
Lessons." *Harvard Management Update*, volume 3, number 11,
4–6.

Webster's New Collegiate Dictionary. 1981. Springfield, MA: G & C
Merriam.

Wiegers, K. "Recognizing Achievements Great and Small." Retrieved
from http://www.processimpact.com/articles/recognize.pdf.

INDEX

A B O U T   T H E   A U T H O R

Renie McClay has managed training for three different *Fortune* 500 companies. She hired, built, managed, and trained sales teams for Kraft. She has led and participated on project teams for corporations and nonprofits. She designs and delivers workshops to build teams, improve communication, and improve team creativity and innovation. She has co-authored *The Essential Guide to Training Global Audiences* (Pfeiffer, 2008) and is the editor of *Sales Training Solutions* and *Fortify Your Sales Force*.

Renie trains and facilitates in person and virtually to audiences in North America, Europe, Africa, Australia, Asia, and Latin America.

THE ASTD MISSION:

Through exceptional learning and performance, we create a world that works better.

The American Society for Training & Development provides world-class professional development opportunities, content, networking, and resources for workplace learning and performance professionals.

Dedicated to helping members increase their relevance, enhance their skills, and align learning to business results, ASTD sets the standard for best practices within the profession.

The society is recognized for shaping global discussions on workforce development and providing the tools to demonstrate the impact of learning on the organizational bottom line. ASTD represents the profession's interests to corporate executives, policy makers, academic leaders, small business owners, and consultants through world-class content, convening opportunities, professional development, and awards and recognition.

Resources
- *T+D (Training + Development)* Magazine
- ASTD Press
- Industry Newsletters
- Research and Benchmarking
- Representation to Policy Makers

Networking
- Local Chapters
- Online Communities
- ASTD Connect
- Benchmarking Forum
- Learning Executives Network

Professional Development
- Certificate Programs
- Conferences and Workshops
- Online Learning
- CPLP™ Certification Through the ASTD Certification Institute
- Career Center and Job Bank

Awards and Best Practices
- ASTD BEST Awards
- Excellence in Practice Awards
- E-Learning Courseware Certification (ECC) Through the ASTD Certification Institute

Learn more about ASTD at www.astd.org.
1.800.628.2783 (U.S.) or 1.703.683.8100
customercare@astd.org

080615.31410

About Berrett-Koehler Publishers

Berrett-Koehler is an independent publisher dedicated to an ambitious mission: Creating a World That Works for All.

We believe that to truly create a better world, action is needed at all levels—individual, organizational, and societal. At the individual level, our publications help people align their lives with their values and with their aspirations for a better world. At the organizational level, our publications promote progressive leadership and management practices, socially responsible approaches to business, and humane and effective organizations. At the societal level, our publications advance social and economic justice, shared prosperity, sustainability, and new solutions to national and global issues.

Visit our website

Go to www.bkconnection.com to read exclusive excerpts of new books, get special discounts, see videos of our authors, read their blogs, find out about author appearances and other BK events, browse our complete catalog, and more!

Get the *BK Communiqué,* our free eNewsletter

News about Berrett-Koehler, yes—new book announcements, special offers, author interviews. But also news by Berrett-Koehler authors, employees, and fellow travelers. Tales of the book trade. Links to our favorite websites and videos—informative, amusing, sometimes inexplicable. Trivia questions—win a free book! Letters to the editor. And much more!

See a sample issue: www.bkconnection.com/BKCommunique.

BK® Berrett–Koehler Publishers, Inc.
San Francisco. *www.bkconnection.com*